GLENCOE
Medical
Terminology
LANGUAGE FOR HEALTH CARE

Joanne Becker, ART
Kirkwood Community College
Cedar Rapids, Iowa

Sarah Galewick, RN, BSN
Redding, California

Nina Thierer, CMA
Ivy Tech State College
Fort Wayne, Indiana

Janette B. Thomas, MPS, RHIA
Professor
State University of New York
College of Technology at Alfred

 **Glencoe McGraw-Hill**

New York, New York   Columbus, Ohio   Woodland Hills, California   Peoria, Illinois

Instructor's Manual for Glencoe *Medical Terminology: Language for Health Care*

Glencoe/McGraw-Hill

A Division of The McGraw·Hill Companies

Co-developed by Glencoe/McGraw-Hill and Chestnut Hill Enterprises, Inc.
Woodbury, Connecticut

Send all inquiries to:
The McGraw-Hill Companies
8787 Orion Place
Columbus, OH 43240-4027

ISBN: 0-02-801290-9

1 2 3 4 5 6 7 8 9 079 06 05 04 03 02 01 00

Contents

Introduction to the Program

Glencoe's *Medical Terminology—Language for Health Care* is designed for use by those students in the allied health curriculum who need to be familiar with medical terms. Its purpose is to provide basic body system knowledge to enable students to build a usable medical vocabulary with an appropriate foundation in word building.

Text

The brief contents of the text is as follows:

Each chapter starts with a set of objectives that outline what goals each student should be able to achieve by the end of that chapter. By studying each section of the chapter, completing the exercises, and performing the chapter review at the end, students should be able to achieve the objectives in a structured manner. The majority of the chapters cover one body system, and the overall effect of the book is to build knowledge of all the body systems and applicable medical terms.

The first three chapters of the book introduce how most medical terms are formed. Most medical terms are built from word parts, most derived from Latin and Greek terms. These three chapters introduce many of the major word parts used in the formation of medical terms. During the study of the first three chapters, students should be introduced to the process of making flash cards (see page viii of this manual). The repetitive use of flash cards has been shown to be extremely effective as a study tool in subjects that require a vocabulary memorization.

Body System Chapters

Chapters 4 through 16 are the body system chapters. Each body system is presented in the following format:

A. Objectives—the major concepts that students should master by the end of the chapter.

B. Structure and Function—the basic anatomy and physiology useful in setting up a basic understanding of the vocabulary being learned and the relationship of the terms to each other.

C. Combining Forms and Abbreviations—the major word parts pertaining specifically to the system being studied.

D. Diagnostic, Procedural, and Laboratory Terms—the most common terms that students might encounter in allied health careers that include exposures to diagnoses, medical procedures, and laboratory tests.

E. Pathological Terms—the most common illnesses of each body system.

F. Surgical Terms—the most common surgical procedures performed for each body system.

G. Pharmacological Terms—an overview of the types of medications with some generic and trade name examples.

H. Challenge Section—an extra situational problem provided for those students who can work on more challenging material.

I. Using the Internet—an exercise designed to familiarize students with the information available on the Internet regarding health care issues.

J. Chapter Review—an overall review of the key terms in the chapter to allow students to test their own mastery of the material.

K. Answer Key—answers to chapter exercises to provide students with instant feedback on their mastery of each chapter section.

Special Features

Each chapter contains special features that reinforce learning, provide additional information, or expose students to realistic situations they may encounter in their chosen allied health professions.

A. Word Analysis—The vocabulary review sections contain a word analysis column of pronunciations and selected word analyses. The word analyses show how certain terms are formed from word parts as well as the etymologies of some words or word parts. The analysis reinforces understanding of how medical terms are built.

B. Case Studies—Throughout the text, case studies present realistic health care situations. Students are exposed to actual medical case histories, some laboratory tests, real diagnoses, health care forms, and medical decision-making. Information in the case studies shows terminology and abbreviations being used in a realistic context.

C. Critical Thinking—Following each case study, students are asked critical thinking questions relating to the case study material and to material learned in the text. Critical-thinking skills are essential to the development of valuable decision-making skills.

D. Picture Boxes—More About boxes appear throughout the book and provide some interesting medical information that would not normally appear within a medical terminology text. Such information adds interest to the study of a subject that requires much repetitive learning.

E. Flowcharts—In most body system chapters at least one flowchart provides a diagrammatic overview of some of the anatomical information. These flowcharts provide a picture of some of the material presented.

Specialized Chapters

Chapters 17 through 22 cover general and special areas of health occupations. Chapter 17, Human Development, presents the stages of the lifespan and the medical terms relating to each stage. Chapter 18 covers oncology in depth. Although cancer of each body system is presented within each body system chapter, students need to learn about the overall structure, causes, treatments, and current understanding of oncology. Specific terminology related to cancer is learned in this chapter. Chapter 19 delves into diagnostic imaging and surgery. As with oncology, imaging and surgery are also covered in each body system chapter. Chapter 19 is an overview of these two subjects as they relate to the terminology needed by today's allied health professionals. Chapter 20 covers terms in psychiatry. Chapter 21 provides an overview of terminology in dental practice. Chapter 22 is an overview of basic pharmacology for the health occupations student.

Instructor's Manual

The *Instructor's Manual to Accompany Medical Terminology—Language for Health Care* is provided to all instructors who adopt the program for use in their classroom. This manual provides numerous teaching suggestions, alternative tests, puzzles, and additional resources.

Making Flash Cards

Flash cards are a useful self-study tool for students. Even the process of making the flash cards is an exercise in memorization. In general, flash cards should have a combining form on one side and the meaning and some examples of words built from that combining form on the other side. Flash cards can be made in a variety of ways. Simple 3×5 index cards provide easy, durable flash cards. Have students write a combining form on one side and the meaning and examples on the other. Index cards are particularly useful for word parts that are unfamiliar to the student. For example, it may not be necessary for a particular student to make a flash card for the combining form *cardio-*, heart, if that is a familiar combining form and the student knows several words formed from it. On the other hand, if the student does not know the form *angio-*, blood vessel, he or she should make a flash card with at least two examples on the back.

For students who need more comprehensive studying, it may be useful to make flash cards for almost all combining forms. Appendix A of the textbook is a list of all the combining forms in the textbook with page references so students can easily find examples. An efficient method of making flash cards is to use a computer to put 6, 8, or 12 words in evenly spaced rectangles on an $8 \ 1/2 \times 11$ sheet of paper. Then key the meaning and two examples of each combining form in even rectangles where they would be positioned on the reverse side of the sheet. If the computer's printer can easily print one side and then, with the paper turned over, the reverse, the student will have sheets of flash cards ready for use. The rectangles can be cut or can be studied in sheets. If not, print the two sides separately and place them together with tape or staples. Sheets of multiple combining forms can also be handwritten in this manner.

Students can use a color-coding method of tracking their own mastery of the flash cards. When students review flash cards, they may put a color highlight in the upper right-hand corner of the cards for those combining forms with which they are familiar and for which they can easily provide two examples. They can then remove all the highlighted flash cards and use them only when doing an overall review. They should concentrate on the other flash cards until all of them are highlighted showing mastery.

Audiotapes

In addition to the textbook, Glencoe also makes audiotapes available. These audiotapes provide pronunciation for each key term in the order that it appears in the body system chapters of the text. Students can study the pronunciations by section as they are learning each section of the chapter. These tapes can also be used as an overall chapter-by-chapter pronunciation review. Instructors who have study labs may make these tapes available for self-study. Students who wish to learn proper pronunciations at home or in their cars may purchase these cassettes for their own use.

Test Bank

A test bank of 2500 questions is available to instructors who adopt the program. Instructions on how to generate tests using *ExamView Pro 3.0* follow.

Section 1—Introduction

This user's guide accompanies a test generator program called *ExamView®
Pro 3.0*—an application that enables you to quickly create printed tests,
Internet tests, and computer (LAN-based) tests. You can enter your own
questions and customize the appearance of the tests you create. The
ExamView Pro test generator program offers many unique features. Using the
QuickTest wizard, for example, you are guided step-by-step through the
process of building a test. Numerous options are included that allow you to
customize the content and appearance of the tests you create.

As you work with the ExamView test generator, you may use the following features:

- **an interview mode or "wizard" to guide you through the steps to
  create a test in less than five minutes**

- **five methods to select test questions**
  - random selection
  - from a list
  - while viewing questions
  - by criteria (difficulty code, objective, topic, etc.—if available)
  - all questions

- **the capability to edit questions or to add an unlimited number of
  questions**

- **online (Internet-based) testing**
  - create a test that students can take on the Internet using a browser
  - receive instant feedback via email
  - create online study guides with student feedback for incorrect
    responses
  - include any of the twelve (12) question types

- **Internet test-hosting ***
  - instantly publish a test to the *ExamView* Website
  - manage tests online
  - allow students to access tests from one convenient location
  - receive detailed reports
  - download results to your gradebook or spreadsheet

- **online (LAN-based) testing**
  - allow anyone or selected students to take a test on your local area
    network
  - schedule tests
  - create online study guides with student feedback for incorrect
    responses
  - incorporate multimedia links (movies and audio)
  - export student results to a gradebook or spreadsheet

- **a sophisticated word processor**
  - streamlined question entry with spell checker
  - tabs, fonts, symbols, foreign characters, and text styles
  - tables with borders and shading
  - full-featured equation editor
  - pictures or other graphics within a question, answer, or narrative

*The Internet test-hosting service must be purchased separately. Visit www.examview.com to learn more.

- **numerous test layout and printing options**
  - scramble the choices in multiple choice questions
  - print multiple versions of the same test with corresponding answer keys
  - print an answer key strip for easier test grading
- **link groups of questions to common narratives**

Section 2—Installation and Startup Instructions

The *ExamView Pro 3.0* test generator software is provided on a CD-ROM or floppy disks. The disk includes the program and all of the questions for the corresponding textbook. The *ExamView Player*, which can be used by your students to take online (computerized or LAN-based) tests, is also included.

Before you can use the test generator, you must install it on your hard drive. The system requirements, installation instructions, and startup procedures are provided below.

System Requirements

To use the *ExamView Pro 3.0* test generator or the online test player, your computer must meet or exceed the following minimum hardware requirements:

Windows

- Pentium computer
- Windows 95, Windows 98, Windows 2000 (or a more recent version)
- color monitor (VGA-compatible)
- CD-ROM and/or high-density floppy disk drive
- hard drive with at least 7 MB space available
- 8 MB available memory (*16 MB memory recommended*)
- an Internet connection to access the Internet test-hosting features

Macintosh

- PowerPC processor, 100 MHz computer
- System 7.5 (or a more recent version)
- color monitor (VGA-compatible)
- CD-ROM and/or high-density floppy disk drive
- hard drive with at least 7 MB space available
- 8 MB available memory (*16 MB memory recommended*)
- an Internet connection with System 8.6 (or more recent version) to access the Internet test-hosting features

Installation Instructions

Follow these steps to install the *ExamView* test generator software. The setup program will automatically install everything you need to use *ExamView*. **Note:** A separate Test Player setup program is also included for your convenience. [See *Installing the Test Player* on page xix for more information.]

Windows

Step 1
Turn on your computer.

Step 2
Insert the *ExamView* disk into the CD-ROM drive. If the program is provided on floppy disks, insert Disk 1 into Drive A.

Step 3
Click the **Start** button on the *Taskbar* and choose the *Run* option.

Step 4
If the *ExamView* software is provided on a CD-ROM, use the drive letter that corresponds to the CD-ROM drive on your computer (e.g., **d:\setup.exe**). The setup program, however, may be located in a subfolder on the CD-ROM if the *ExamView* software is included on the disk with other resources. In which case, click the **Browse** button in the Run dialog box to locate the setup program (e.g., **d:\evpro\setup.exe**).

If you are installing the software from floppy disks, type **a:\setup** and press **Enter** to run the installation program.

Step 5
Follow the prompts on the screen to complete the installation process.

If the software and question banks are provided on more than one floppy disk, you will be prompted to insert the appropriate disk when it is needed.

Step 6
Remove the installation disk when you finish.

Macintosh

Step 1
Turn on your computer.

Step 2
Insert the *ExamView* installation disk into your CD-ROM drive. If the program is provided on floppy disks, insert Disk 1 into a disk drive.

Step 3
Open the installer window, if necessary.

Step 4
Double-click the installation icon to start the program.

Step 5
Follow the prompts on the screen to complete the installation process.

If the software and question banks are provided on more than one floppy disk, you will be prompted to insert the appropriate disk when it is needed.

Step 6
Remove the installation disk when you finish.

Getting Started

After you complete the installation process, follow these instructions to start the *ExamView* test generator software. This section also explains the options used to create a test and edit a question bank.

Startup Instructions

Step 1
Turn on the computer.

Step 2
Windows: Click the **Start** button on the *Taskbar*. Highlight the **Programs** menu and locate the *ExamView Test Generator* folder. Select the *ExamView Pro* option to start the software.

Macintosh: Locate and open the *ExamView* folder. Double-click the *ExamView Pro* program icon.

Step 3
The first time you run the software you will be prompted to enter your name, school/institution name, and city/state. You are now ready to begin using the *ExamView* software.

Step 4
Each time you start *ExamView*, the **Startup** menu appears. Choose one of the options shown in Figure 1. **Note:** All of the figures shown in this user's guide are taken from the Windows software. Except for a few minor differences, the Macintosh screens are identical.

Step 5
Use *ExamView* to create a test or edit questions in a question bank.

    ExamView includes three components: Test Builder, Question Bank Editor, and Test Player. The **Test Builder** includes options to create, edit, print, and save tests. The **Question Bank Editor** lets you create or edit question banks. The **Test Player** is a separate program that your students can use to take online (LAN-based) tests/study guides.

Figure 1—ExamView Startup Menu

Using The Help System

Whenever you need assistance using *ExamView*, access the extensive help system. Click the **Help** button or choose the **Help Topics** option from the *Help* menu to access step-by-step instructions from more than 150 help topics. If you experience any difficulties while you are working with the software, you may want to review the troubleshooting tips in the user-friendly help system.

Test Builder

The Test Builder allows you to create tests using the QuickTest Wizard or you can create a new test on your own. (See the sample test in Figure 2.) Use the Test Builder to prepare both printed and online tests/study guides.

- *If you want ExamView to select questions randomly from one or more question banks,* choose the *QuickTest Wizard* option to create a new test. (Refer to Figure 1 on page xii.) Then, follow the step-by-step instructions to (1) enter a test title, (2) choose one or more question banks from which to select questions, and (3) identify how many questions you want on the test. The QuickTest Wizard will automatically create a new test and use the Test Builder to display the test on screen. You can print the test as is, remove questions, add new questions, or edit any question.

- *If you want to create a new test on your own,* choose the option to create a new test. (Refer to Figure 1 on page xii.) Then identify a question bank from which to choose questions by using the *Question Bank* option in the **Select** menu. You may then add questions to the test by using one or more of the following selection options: *Randomly, From a List, While Viewing, By Criteria,* or *All Questions*.

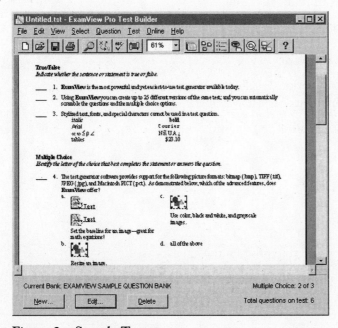

Figure 2—Sample Test

IMPORTANT: The Test Builder and the Question Bank Editor systems are integrated in one program. As you work with *ExamView*, you can easily switch between the Test Builder and Question Bank Editor components using the *Switch to...* option in the **File** menu.

To create a new test:

Step 1
Start the *ExamView* software.

Step 2
At the Startup window, choose the *Create a new test* option.

Step 3
Enter a title for the new test.

After you enter the title, the program will automatically display the option for you to select a question bank.

Step 4
Choose a question bank.

Step 5
Select the questions you want to include on the test.

Use the question selection options that appear in the **Select** menu. Or, click the corresponding buttons on the toolbar. A description for each of the question selection toolbar buttons appears below.

Click the **Question Bank** toolbar button to select a question bank. You can create a test using questions from one question bank or from multiple banks. Choose a bank, select the questions you want, and then choose another bank to select more questions.

Click the **Select Randomly** toolbar button when you want the program to randomly select questions for you.

Use the **Select from a List** command to choose questions if you know which ones you want to select. Identify the questions you want by reviewing a question bank printout.

Click the **Select while Viewing** button to display a window that shows all of the questions in the current question bank. Click the check boxes to select the questions you want.

You can use the **Select by Criteria** option to choose questions based on question type, difficulty, and objective (if available).

Click the **Select All** button to choose all of the questions in the current question bank.

Step 6
Save the test.

Step 7
Print the test.

You can use the options in the **Test** menu to customize the appearance of a test, edit test instructions, and choose to leave space for students to write their answers. When you print a test, you may choose how many variations of the test you want, whether you want all the versions to be the same, and whether you want to scramble the questions and the multiple choice options. If you choose to scramble the questions, *ExamView* will print a custom answer sheet for each variation of the test.

If you want your students to take a test online, first create the test. Then, publish the test as an Internet test/study guide (page xxiv) or use the Online Test Wizard (page xviii) to create a test for delivery over a LAN (local area network). The software will walk you through the steps to turn any test into an online (Internet or LAN-based) test.

IMPORTANT: You may edit questions or create new questions as you build your test. However, those questions can be used only as part of the current test. If you plan to create several new questions that you would like to use on other tests, switch to the Question Bank Editor to add the new questions.

Question Bank Editor

The Question Bank Editor allows you to edit questions in an existing publisher-supplied question bank or to create your own new question banks. Always use the Question Bank Editor if you want to change a question permanently in an existing question bank. If you want to make a change that applies only to a particular test, create a new question or edit that question in the Test Builder.

A question bank may include up to 250 questions in a variety of formats including multiple choice, true/false, modified true/false, completion, yes/no, matching, problem, essay, short answer, case, and numeric response. You can include the following information for each question: difficulty code, reference, text objective, state objectives, topic, and notes.

Step 1
Start the *ExamView* software.

Step 2
At the Startup window as illustrated in Figure 1 on page xii, choose to *Create a new question bank* or *Open an existing question bank*.

If you are working in the Test Builder, click the **File** menu and choose *Switch to Question Bank Editor* to edit or create a new question bank.

Step 3
Click the **New** button to create a new question or click the **Edit** button to modify an existing question. Both of these buttons appear at the bottom of the Question Bank Editor window. (See Figure 3 on p. xvi.)

You may add new questions or edit questions in a question bank by using the built-in word processor. The word processor includes many features commonly found in commercially available word processing applications. These features include the following: fonts, styles, tables, paragraph formatting, ruler controls, tabs, indents, and justification.

Step 4
Save your work. Then, exit the program or switch back to the Test Builder.

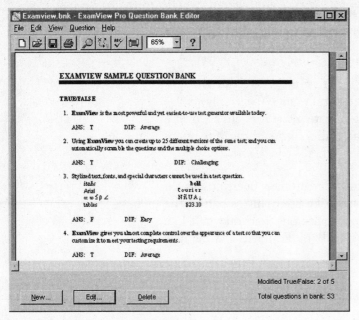

Figure 3—Question Bank Editor

Online Testing (LAN-based vs. Internet)

The *ExamView* software allows you to create paper tests and online tests. The program provides two distinct online testing options: **LAN-based** testing and **Internet** testing. The option you choose depends on your particular testing needs. You can choose either option to administer online tests and study guides.

The **LAN-based** testing option is designed to work on a local area network server. That is, you can copy the test/study guide along with the Test Player software onto your local area network. Then students can take the test at computers connected to your server.

To take a LAN-based test you must provide access for your students to the Test Player program included with the *ExamView* software. The Test Player is a separate program that lets your students take a test/study guide at a computer. You can store the Test Player program and the test on a local area network for easy access by your students.

The **Internet** testing option provides a computerized testing solution for delivering tests via the Internet or an Intranet. This option is great for distance learning environments or simply to make a sample test/study guide available to students at home. Students do not need any other program (unlike the LAN-based option). When your students take a test, the results are automatically sent to you via email.

You can publish an Internet test to your own Website, or you can use the *ExamView* Internet test-hosting service. If you subscribe to the *ExamView* test-hosting service, you can publish a test directly to the Internet with just a few simple steps. Students will have immediate access to the tests that you publish and you can get detailed reports. For more information on the Internet test-hosting service, visit our website at www.examview.com.

Section 3—Online (LAN-based) Testing

Online testing features are seamlessly integrated into the *ExamView* software. If you want to take advantage of these capabilities, simply create a test and then use the Online Test Wizard to setup the testing parameters. Students can then take the test at the computer using the Test Player program.

IMPORTANT: If you want to prepare a test/study guide for delivery via the Internet, use the *Publish Internet Test* option as described on page xxiv.

ExamView includes many features that let you customize an online (LAN-based) test. You can create a test for a specific class, or you can prepare a study guide for anyone to take. Using the Online Test Wizard, you can schedule a test or allow it to be taken anytime. As your students work on a test, *ExamView* will scramble the question order, provide feedback for incorrect responses, and display a timer if you selected any of these options.

Online (LAN-based) Testing Overview

Refer to the steps below for an overview of the online (LAN-based) testing process. Specific instructions for creating a test, taking a test, and viewing results are provided on the following pages.

Step 1
Talk with your network administrator to help you setup a location (folder) on your local area network where you can install the Test Player software and copy your tests/study guides.

Make sure that the administrator gives you and your students full access to the designated folders on the server. You may also want your network administrator to install the Test Player software.

Step 2
Create a test/study guide, and then use the Online Test Wizard to setup the online (LAN-based) test. Save your work and exit the *ExamView* software.

Step 3
Transfer the test/study guide file [e.g., chapter1.tst (Windows) or Chapter 1 (Macintosh)] and any accompanying multimedia files from your computer to the local area network server.

Copy the files from your hard drive to the folder setup by your network administrator. You need only copy the test file unless you linked an audio or video segment to one or more questions.

Step 4
Instruct your students to complete the test/study guide.

Students must have access to a computer connected to the local area network on which the Test Player and test/study guide are stored.

Step 5
After all students finish taking the test, copy the test/study guide file back to your hard drive. It is recommended that you copy the test to a different location from the original test file. The test file, itself, contains all of the students' results.

Note: If you set up a class roster, the test file will contain item analysis information and the results for each student. If you did not setup a roster, no results are recorded so you do not have to complete this step or the next.

Step 6
Start the *ExamView* software and open the test file to view your students' results.

Creating an Online (LAN-based) Test

Follow the steps shown below to create an online (LAN-based) test or study guide. Depending on the options you set, you can create a test or study guide. Before you begin, make sure that you installed the *ExamView* test generator and Test Player software. **Note:** See the next section (page xix) for instructions to setup the Test Player. (See page xxiii for Internet testing features.)

Step 1
Start the *ExamView* software.

Step 2
Create or open a test/study guide.

Select the questions you want to include on the test. You can include any of the following types: True/False, Multiple Choice, Yes/No, Numeric Response, Completion, and Matching.

Step 3
Select the *Online Test Wizard* option from the **Online** menu.

ExamView presents step-by-step instructions to help you prepare the online test/study guide. (See Figure 4.) Read the instructions provided

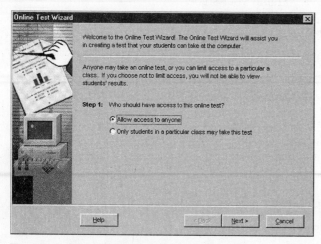

Figure 4—Online Test Wizard (Step 1)

and complete each step. **Note:** Click the **Help** button if you need more assistance.

Step 4
Click the **Finish** button after you complete the last step using the Online Test Wizard. As you can see in Figure 5 on page xix, *ExamView* shows a summary that describes the settings for the online test.

Step 5
Save the test/study guide to a location where your students can easily access it. For example, save it in the same location where you installed the Test Player program.

It is recommended that you save the test/study guide to a location on a network server where students have read/write access. The Test Player will store all of your students' results (if you entered a class roster) in the test file itself. You can copy the test to individual computers, but this configuration takes more time to gather the results.

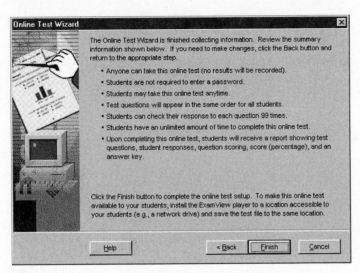

Figure 5—Online Test Wizard (Summary)

Step 6
If you included multimedia links in any of the questions, copy those files to the same location where you saved the test/study guide.

If the multimedia files are on a CD-ROM or DVD disk, you may leave them on the disk, but provide this information to your students. To play one of these links, they will have to specify the location of the multimedia file.

NOTES:
- Use the *Test Preferences* and *Class Roster* options in the **Online** menu if you want to make any changes to the test parameters. These two options let you change any of the settings you selected using the Online Test Wizard.
- You must close the test before your students can access it with the Test Player.
- If you setup a class roster for a test/study guide, you cannot modify the test (e.g., edit a question, change the order, etc.) once any student has taken it unless you clear the results first.
- Provide your students with the Test Player setup program and a copy of the test/study guide if you want them to take it at home.

Installing the Test Player

Follow the instructions provided here to install the Test Player program for your students. You may copy the Test Player to a network (recommended), install it on individual computers, or provide it on floppy disks for your students to take home.

Even if you have a network, you can install the Test Player on individual computers. Students will still be able to access tests/study guides you store on a local area network.

ExamView Player Installation

Step 1
Turn on your computer.

Step 2
Insert the *ExamView* disk into your CD-ROM drive. If the software was provided on floppy disks, insert the *ExamView–Test Player* installation disk into Drive A.

Step 3
Click the **Start** button on the *Taskbar* and choose the *Run* option.

Step 4
If the *ExamView* software is provided on a CD-ROM, use the drive letter that corresponds to the CD-ROM drive on your computer (e.g., **d:\evplayer\setup** or **d:\evpro\evplayer\setup**).

    If you are installing the software from a floppy disk, type **a:\setup** and press **Enter** to run the installation program.

Step 5
When prompted for a location to install the program, select a folder (e.g., **x:\programs\evplayer** for network installations or **c:\evplayer** on your local hard drive).

Step 6
For local area network (**LAN**) installations, complete the following steps at each workstation:

- Click the **Start** button and choose **Taskbar** from the *Settings* menu.
- Click the **Start Menu Programs** tab and click **Add**.
- Type the location and program name for the Test Player software, or use the **Browse** button to enter this information (e.g., **x:\programs\evplayer\evplayer.exe**).
- Proceed to the next screen and add a new folder (e.g., **ExamView Test Player**).
- Enter **ExamView Test Player** as the shortcut name and then click the **Finish** button.

Repeat Steps 1–5 if you plan to install the software at each computer instead of installing the program once on your network.

Step 1
Turn on your computer.

Step 2
Insert the *ExamView* installation disk into your CD-ROM drive. If the program is provided on floppy disks, insert the *ExamView–Test Player* installation disk into a disk drive.

Step 3
Open the installer window, if necessary.

Step 4

Double-click the installation icon to start the program.

    Note: The installation program is configured to copy the test player to a new folder on your hard drive. You can, however, change this location. For example, you can select a location on your network server.

Step 5

When prompted for a location to install the program, select a folder on your local area network that is accessible to all students. If you are installing the software on a stand-alone computer, choose a location on the hard drive.

Step 6

At each workstation, enable file sharing and program linking if you installed the application on your network server.

    For stand-alone computers, repeat Steps 1–5.

Installing the Test Player at Home

You can give your students the Test Player software to take home. If the *ExamView* software was sent to you on floppy disks, give your students the separate Test Player setup disk. If you received the software on CD-ROM, copy all of the setup files in the *evplayer* folder onto a floppy disk. Students should follow Steps 1–5 to install the software on their computer. When a student takes a test home, he/she should copy it into the same folder as the Test Player program.

Taking an Online (LAN-based) Test

Make sure that you have properly installed the *ExamView* Test Player software and copied the test/study guide to a location easily accessible to your students. If you linked multimedia files to any of the questions, it is recommended that you copy those files to the same folder as the test/study guide.

    If you created a test with a class roster, students must correctly enter their ID's to be able to take the test/study guide. Provide this information to your students, if necessary. **Note:** If you do not want to track student scores, you should set up a test to allow anyone to take it.

    Step 1

Start the *ExamView* Test Player software.

    Step 2

Enter your name and ID. (See Figure 6 on p. xxii.)

    Step 3

Select a test/study guide. (See Figure 7 on p. xxii.)

    If no tests (or study guides) appear in the list, click the **Folder** button to identify where the tests are located.

    Step 4

(Optional) Enter a password, if prompted.

    Step 5

Review the summary information and click **Start** when you are ready to begin.

    Step 6

Answer all of the questions and click the **End** button when you finish.

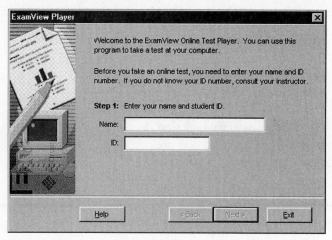

Figure 6—Online Test/Study Guide Registration

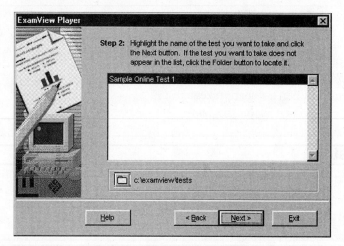

Figure 7—Online Test/Study Guide Selection

Verify that you want to end the test. If you do not answer all of the questions in one session, you will *not* be able to resume the test at a later time.

Step 7
Review the test report.

Step 8
Click **New Test** to take another test or click **Exit** to quit the program.

Viewing Online (LAN-based) Results

If you set up a test with a class roster (instead of allowing anyone to access a test/study guide), the *ExamView* Test Player will automatically collect the results for each student. The program saves this information in the test/study guide file itself.

Step 1
Start the *ExamView* software and open the online test/study guide that your students have already taken.

Step 2

Choose *View Test Results* from the **Online** menu.

Step 3

Review the results, item-by-item analysis, and statistics reports.

Step 4

Choose *Export Test Results* if you want to export the scores to your favorite gradebook program or spreadsheet application.

Section 4—Internet Testing

ExamView lets you easily create Internet tests and study guides. Build a test and then simply choose the *Publish Internet Test* option. You can choose to post tests to your own Website, or publish tests directly to the *ExamView* Website. (Visit us at www.examview.com to learn more about subscribing to the Internet test-hosting service.)

With the Internet test-hosting feature, you can publish a test or study guide directly to the *ExamView* Website. Simply create a test and then follow the easy step-by-step instructions to publish it to the Internet. It's that simple! You can manage tests online, view reports, and download results. Students access your tests from one convenient location.

If you do not use the ExamView test-hosting service, you can manually post tests/study guides to your own Website. If you create a test, your students' results are sent to you via email automatically. Or, you can create a study guide that your students can use to review various topics at their own pace.

Internet Testing FAQs

Review the FAQs (frequently asked questions) below for more information on the Internet testing hosting features available to *ExamView Pro 3.0* users.

What are the advantages to using the Internet test-hosting feature? (1) Publishing an Internet test to your own Website and setting up links can be quite challenging. With the Internet test-hosting feature, the process is completely automated. In minutes, you can post a test to the Internet. (2) When you post tests/study guides to your own Website, only a few options are available. Using the *ExamView* test-hosting service, you have many more options available such as setting up a class roster and viewing detailed item analysis reports.

How do you register for the test-hosting service? Visit our Website at www.examview.com to learn how to register. Before you can post tests/study guides, you must sign up to obtain a valid instructor ID and a password.

Is there an additional charge for the Internet test-hosting service? Yes, there is an additional yearly subscription charge to use this service. If you received the *ExamView* software from a publisher, you may be eligible for a discount or a free trial membership. (See our Website for current prices and special promotions.)

Do you have to use the Internet test-hosting service? No, using the test-hosting service is not required. The Publish Internet Test feature includes an option to save an Internet test/study guide to a local hard drive. Then, you can manually post it to your own Website.

Why aren't the same features available for tests posted to my own Website? To offer the numerous Internet test-hosting features, we have developed many programs and databases that are stored on our servers. If you post to your own server or Website, these programs are not available.

IMPORTANT: Your students must use a browser such as Netscape 4.0/Internet Explorer 4.0 (or a more recent version) that supports cascading style sheets (CSS1) and JavaScript. To post tests or study guides for delivery via the Internet, you must have your own access to an Internet server.

Using the Internet Test-Hosting Service

Using the *ExamView* test generator software you can publish tests directly to the *ExamView* Website if you have signed up for the test-hosting service. With a few simple steps, you can publish tests and study guides directly to the Internet. Refer to the following instructions to: register for the Internet test-hosting service, create a test, publish a test to the Internet, take tests online, manage tests, and view student results.

Register for the Internet Test-Hosting Service

Step 1
Launch your Web browser and go to www.examview.com.

Step 2
Go to the **Instructor Center** to register for the test-hosting service. Follow the instructions provided at the Website to sign up.

Record the instructor ID and password assigned to you. You will need this information to publish a test or study guide to the *ExamView* Website. When you choose to publish a test, you will be prompted to enter this information.

Step 3
Quit the browser.

Publish a Test/Study Guide to the ExamView Website

Step 1
Start the *ExamView* software.

Step 2
Create a new test or open an existing test.

Select the questions you want to include on the test. You can include any of the twelve (12) question types on a test, but only the objective questions are scored.

Step 3
Select the *Publish Internet Test* option from the **File** menu.

ExamView presents a window with various Internet testing options to help you prepare the online test. (See Figure 8.) **Note:** Click the Help button if you need more assistance.

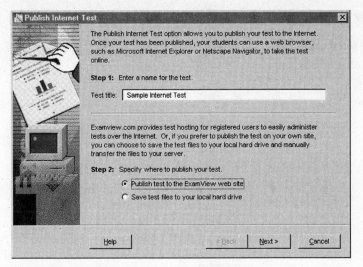

Figure 8—Publish Internet Test Window

Step 4
Name the test.

Step 5
Select the option to publish your test to the *ExamView* Website, and then click the **Next** button.

Step 6
Enter your instructor ID and password.

If you do not already have an instructor ID and password, click the **Register Now** button to launch your Web browser and go to the www.examview.com Website. You cannot proceed until you have a valid instructor ID and password.

Step 7
Choose whether you want to publish a test or a study guide.

Step 8
Specify when students may access the test/study guide.

Step 9
Enter the expiration date.

Step 10
Specify who should have access to this test/study guide.

Anyone may take it, or you may limit access to a particular group of students. If you specify a roster, students must enter an ID and password.

Step 11
Enter a student password, and click **Next.**

Step 12
Review the summary information. Click the **Back** button if you need to make changes. (See Figure 9 or p. xxvi.)

Step 13
Click the **Publish** button when you are ready to post the test/study guide to the *ExamView* Website.

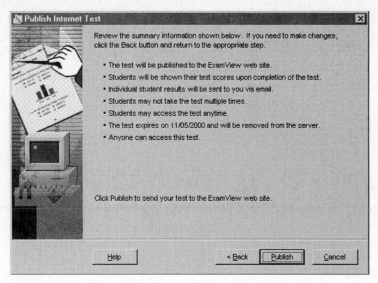

Figure 9—Publish Internet Test Window (Summary)

The program automatically connects to the Internet and posts the test/study guide to the *ExamView* server. Access the instructor options on the *ExamView* Website (www.examview.com) to preview a test, change selected parameters, or view results. If you need to edit or delete questions, you must change the test locally and then publish a new version. **Note:** An Internet connection is required to publish a test/study guide.

Step 14
Print a copy of the test/study guide for your records, create another test, or exit the software if you are finished.

Take a Test/Study Guide Online at www.evtestcenter.com

Once you publish a test/study guide to the *ExamView* server, anyone in the world can access it if you provide him or her with your instructor ID and the appropriate password. (**IMPORTANT:** *Do **not** give students your password, just your ID.*) Provide the instructions below to your students so that they can take the test or study guide.

Note: You must use a browser such as Netscape 4.0/Internet Explorer 4.0 (or a more recent version) that supports cascading style sheets level 1 (CSS1) and JavaScript. An active Internet connection is also required.

To take a test:
Step 1
Start your Web browser.

Step 2
Go to the URL: www.evtestcenter.com.

Step 3
Enter your instructor's ID code. (See Figure 10.)
Upon entering a valid instructor code, you will see a list of tests your instructor has published.

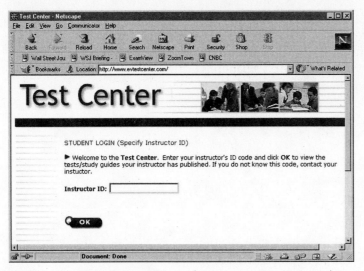

Figure 10—Test Center Login (www.evtestcenter.com)

Step 4
Select a test.

Step 5
Enter your name (if requested), student ID, and password.

Contact your instructor if you have not been assigned a student ID or you do not have a password.

Step 6
Review the test and respond to all of the questions. (See the sample test in Figure 11.)

If you need help while working with a test, click the **Help** button shown at the bottom of the test. Click the browser's **Back** button to return to the test.

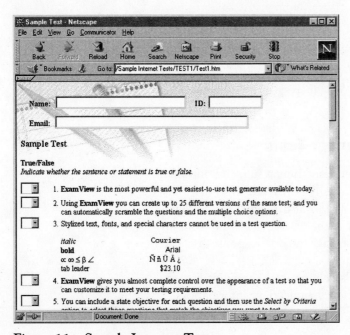

Figure 11—Sample Internet Test

Step 7

When you complete the test, review the entire test and then click the **Grade & Submit** button located at the bottom of the test.

Your results will be emailed to your instructor. Depending on the test settings, you may be notified of your results immediately.

To complete a study guide:

Step 1

Start your Web browser.

Step 2

Go to the URL: www.evtestcenter.com.

Step 3

Enter your instructor's ID.

You will see a list of study guides and tests your instructor has published.

Step 4

Select a study guide.

Step 5

Enter your name (if requested), student ID, and password.

Contact your instructor if you have not been assigned a student ID or you do not have a password.

Step 6

Review the study guide and answer all of the questions.

If you need help while working with a study guide, click the **Help** button shown at the bottom of the screen. Click the browser's **Back** button to return to the study guide.

Step 7

When you complete the study guide, review your responses and then click the **Check Your Work** button located at the bottom of the study guide.

Your work is scored and you will see whether you answered each question correctly or incorrectly. No results are sent to your instructor.

Step 8

Click the **Reset** button to erase all of your responses if you want to start over.

Review Student Results and Manage Tests

When your students complete an Internet test, their results are automatically stored on the server so that you can easily access this information. If you chose to receive results via email, you will also receive the following information for each student: (1) student name and ID, (2) raw score and percentage score for objective-based questions, and (3) responses for each question (objective and open-ended questions).

At the *ExamView* Website, you may also change test-setup options, preview tests, download student results, and view your account information.

Step 1

Start your Web browser.

Step 2

Go to the URL: www.examview.com and access the Instructor Center.

Step 3

Log in using your instructor ID and password to view the main menu options. (See Figure 12.)

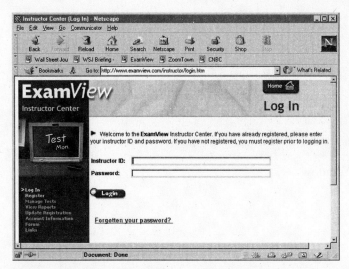

Figure 12—*ExamView* Website (Instructor Center)

Publishing Tests to Your Own Website

If you choose not to sign up for the *ExamView* test-hosting service, you can still publish tests/study guides to your own Website. You must save the test/study guide to your hard drive, upload the files to your Website, and then provide access to your students. Refer to the following sections for step-by-step instructions.

Save an Internet Test/Study Guide to Your Hard Drive

Follow the steps shown below to create an Internet test/study guide and save it to your hard drive. Before you begin, make sure that you installed the *ExamView* test generator software.

Step 1

Start the *ExamView* software.

Step 2

Create a new test or open an existing test.

Select the questions you want to include on the test. You can include any of the twelve (12) question types on a test, but only the objective questions will be graded.

Step 3

Select the *Publish Internet Test* option from the **File** menu.

ExamView presents a window with various Internet testing options to help you prepare the online test. (See Figure 13.) **Note:** Click the **Help** button if you need more assistance.

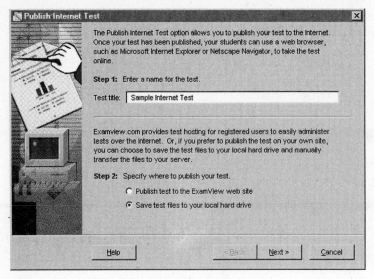

Figure 13—Publish Internet Test Window

Step 4
Name the test.

Step 5
Select the option to save the test files to your local hard drive, and then click the **Next** button.

Step 6
Choose whether you want to publish a test or a study guide.

Step 7
Review the summary information. Make changes, if necessary.

Step 8
Click the **Save** button to save the test/study guide files.

When you choose to save an Internet test to your local hard drive, *ExamView* creates an HTML file and an accompanying folder with all of the necessary image files. This makes it easier for you to post the files to a Web server. If, for example, you enter a path such as **c:\examview\tests\chapter1** (Windows) or **HD:ExamView: Tests:Chapter1** (Macintosh), the software will create a file called **chapter1.htm** and a new folder called **chapter1_files** with all of the required picture files. (See the illustration below.)

Step 9
Post the test/study guide to a server to make it available to your students. (See the next section for instructions for posting a test to a server.)

Step 10

Once you post a test, you should verify that students can access it. You may also want to try the "Grade & Submit" feature for tests to make sure that the results are emailed to the correct address.

Note: When you create a test, *ExamView* encrypts the answer information so that a student cannot see the answers in the HTML page source. While this does help to prevent cheating, there is no foolproof method in an unsupervised environment.

Post a Test to Your own Internet/Intranet Server

Once you save a test/study guide formatted for the Internet, you must post all of the related files to a location on a server that your students can access. You can post the files to a local area network, Intranet server, or an Internet server. You *must* have an Internet connection for students to be able to submit test results. (This is not required for a study guide.)

Note: Posting to a server can be a complex process. The specific steps will vary depending on the hardware and software configuration of your server. If you are not familiar with the required steps, contact your network administrator for assistance.

Step 1

Start an FTP program or other utility that allows you to copy files from your hard drive to an Internet/Intranet server.

Step 2

Log in to your server.

Step 3

Create a new folder on your server to hold the test/study guide files.

Step 4

Copy the **HTML** file and the accompanying folder to a location on your server that your students can access.

   When you choose to save an Internet test to your hard drive, *ExamView* creates an HTML file and an accompanying folder with all of the necessary image files. This makes it easier for you to post the files to a Web server.

IMPORTANT: By default, all of the file names are lowercase. Do not change the case since these files are referenced in the HTML document. You *must* copy the HTML file and the accompanying folder as is. Do not copy the HTML file into the corresponding folder. (See the illustration below.)

Step 5

Log off the server, if necessary.

Step 6

Record the URL for the test/study guide HTML document or set up a link to the test.

Take a Test or Study Guide Using the Internet

Once you post a test on a server, anyone in the world can access the test if you provide him or her with the Web (URL) address. Follow the instructions provided below to take a test or study guide.

Note: You must use a browser such as Netscape 4.0/Internet Explorer 4.0 (or a more recent version) that supports cascading style sheets level 1 (CSS1) and JavaScript. An active Internet connection is required to submit test results.

To take a test via the Internet:

Step 1
Start your Web browser.

Step 2
Type the Web address (URL) and test name (e.g., **www.school.edu\economics\test1.htm**), or enter an address for a page with a link to the test. (See the sample test in Figure 14.)

If the test is located on a local area network, use the open page command in the browser to open the test.

Step 3
Enter your name, student ID, and email address (optional).

Step 4
Answer all of the questions.

If you need help while working with a test, click the **Help** button shown at the bottom of the test. Click the browser's **Back** button to return to the test.

Step 5
When you complete the test, review your responses and then click the **Grade & Submit** button located at the bottom of the screen.

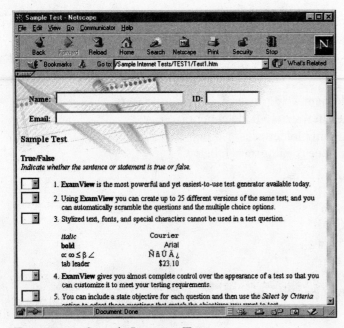

Figure 14—Sample Internet Test

To complete a study guide via the Internet:

Step 1
Start your Web browser.

Step 2
Type the Web address (URL) and study guide name (e.g., **www.school.edu\history\study.htm**), or enter an address for a page with a link to the study guide.

Step 3
Enter your name.

Step 4
Answer all of the questions.

Step 5
When you complete the study guide, review the entire test and then click the **Check Your Work** button located at the bottom of the study guide.

Your work is scored and you will see whether you answered each question correctly or incorrectly. No results are sent to your instructor.

Step 6
Click the **Reset** button to erase all of your responses if you want to start over.

Receive Student Results via Email

When your students complete an Internet test, the browser sends the students' test results and all of their responses directly to you via email. The email will include the following information:

- student name and ID
- raw score and percentage score for objective-based questions
- responses for each question (objective and open-ended questions)

Note: **You will not receive any student results for Internet study guides.**

CD-ROM

The Glencoe Medical Terminology CD-ROM is an interactive tutorial designed to complement the student textbook. In it you will find key terms, flash cards, drag and drop word building and labeling exercises, and games designed to challenge you, such as Hangman and That's Epidemic.

System Requirements

To run this product, your computer must meet the following *minimum* specifications:

1. Pentium processor
2. Windows 95 or Windows 98
3. 32 MB RAM (64 recommended)
4. Desktop screen area set to 800 × 600 or higher

5. Desktop colors set to 16-bit (high color) or higher

6. 16-bit sound card with speakers or headphones (optional)

7. Microphone (optional)

8. Internet Explorer 5.0 or appropriate system files installed. This product does not use Internet Explorer, but it depends on many of the same system files that Internet Explorer uses.

Installation

The installation program checks your computer to confirm that it meets the minimum specifications to run this program.

If you do not have Microsoft Internet Explorer 5.0 or higher installed, the setup program should detect this and direct you to the Internet Explorer setup located on the CD-ROM. If you need to run the Internet Explorer setup, go to the **IEsetup** folder and run the "setup.exe" file. Once the Internet Explorer setup is complete, you will need to re-run the setup for this program.

To run the setup program:

1. Insert the CD-ROM in your CD-ROM drive.

2. If your CD-ROM drive has Auto Insert Notification active, a dialog box will appear automatically, asking if you would like to install this program. Click OK to begin installation.

3. If your CD-ROM drive does not have Auto Insert Notification active, go to your Windows Start menu, select "Run" and type D:\setup.exe in the dialog box (where D: is the letter of your CD-ROM drive). Click OK and follow the instructions that appear.

4. The installation program will create a Windows program group called Glencoe Medical Terminology. In that program group you will find a program icon and an uninstall icon. To start the program, go to the Windows Start Menu > Programs > Glencoe Medical Terminology > Glencoe Medical Terminology (program icon).

Changing the Desktop Setting

If your desktop screen area is 640 × 480, you must re-set it to 800 × 600 or higher. You can do this yourself by opening the Windows Control Panel and double-clicking the "Display" icon. (A shortcut to this dialog box is to right-click anywhere on the desktop and select "Properties" from the pop-up menu that appears.)

From the "Display Properties" dialog box that appears, select the "Settings" tab. Move the "Screen Area" slider to select the "800 × 600" option, and click "OK" to accept this change. You may have to restart your computer for the new settings to take effect.

Changing the Color Setting

For best graphics performance, your computer's color setting should be set to high color (16-bit). To change your color setting, go to the "Display Properties" dialog (from the Windows Control Panel, or by right-clicking the desktop and selecting "Properties"). From the "Colors" drop-down box, select "High Color (16 bit)" and click OK. You may have to restart your computer for the new settings to take effect.

The Help Section

Once you have installed the software, you are strongly encouraged to read and review the Help section of this software. The Help section will explain in detail all of the features and activities of this software. It will also discuss frequently asked questions and offer troubleshooting tips. To access help, click the ? icon found on the top right of your computer screen.

POWERPOINT

The Instructor Presentation Software is located on the CD-ROM that accompanies this Instructor's Manual. It contains PowerPoint presentations for the twenty-two chapters of *Glencoe Medical Terminology—Language for Health Care*. These presentations summarize the chapter material, including the figures. The CD-ROM also contains the PowerPoint Viewer, which is a program used to run slide shows on computers that do not have the full PowerPoint program installed.

If you have PowerPoint 97 (or higher), it is not necessary to install the PowerPoint Viewer in order to view the slides. Also, PowerPoint 97 can be used to modify the prepared presentations if desired.

PowerPoint Viewer Installation Instructions

To install the PowerPoint Viewer, use the following instructions. Note that Windows 95 or higher is required to run the PowerPoint Viewer. Also, a display setting of 640 × 480 or 800 × 600 is strongly recommended.

1. Insert the CD-ROM into the CD-ROM drive on your computer.

2. Click START and then RUN.

3. Key E:\PPVIEW97 and press ENTER. (Note: Use the appropriate drive letter corresponding to the CD-ROM drive on your computer.)

4. Follow the on-screen instructions to complete the installation process. (Note: The PowerPoint Viewer must be installed on the hard drive.)

Start-up Instructions

Use the following instructions to load and view the PowerPoint presentations:

1. Insert the CD-ROM into the CD-ROM drive on your computer.

2. If you are using Windows 98, the presentation may open automatically to a menu of the chapters in *Glencoe Medical Terminology*. If not, click START and then RUN, and key E:\START.EXE and press ENTER. (Note: Use the appropriate drive letter corresponding to the CD-ROM drive on your computer.)

Using the PowerPoint Presentation

To view the PowerPoint presentation for a particular chapter, click the chapter and PowerPoint will load the presentation. (Click HELP for additional instructions.) While viewing the presentation, press the SPACE BAR to move to the next slide or click the left mouse button. Use the PgUp key to return to the slide previously viewed.

To exit the PowerPoint slide show, press the ESC key. Note: Do not remove the CD-ROM from the CD-ROM drive while the program is running; this will cause the system to crash. Always completely exit the PowerPoint presentation.

Modifying the PowerPoint Presentation

If you have PowerPoint 97 (or higher), you will be able to modify the prepared presentation. Begin by pressing the ESC key. Save your changes by clicking FILE, SAVE AS, and saving the presentation (.ppt) from the CD-ROM drive to the hard drive.

SCANS

The U.S. Department of Labor developed the SCANS (Secretary's Commission on Achieving Necessary Skills) goals in order to reflect the need for the United States to develop and maintain a competitive workforce. These goals are accomplished through specific competencies and foundations developed by SCANS. The competencies aim to have students think through problems on their own, make reasonable decisions, and implement these decisions with specific goals in mind. The chart below correlates the competencies with this program.

SCANS (Secretary's Commission on Achieving Necessary Skills) Correlation Chart

Competencies	Text Chapters
I. RESOURCES: Identifies, organizes, plans, and allocates resources	1–22
A. *Time*—Selects goal-relevant activities, ranks them, allocates time, and prepares and follows schedules	
B. *Money*—Uses or prepares budgets, keeps records, and makes adjustments to meet objectives	
C. *Material and Facilities*—Acquires, stores, allocates, and uses materials or space efficiently	
D. *Human Resources*—Assesses skills and distributes work accordingly; evaluates performance and provides feedback	
II. INTERPERSONAL: Works with others	1, 4–22
A. *Participates as Member of a Team*—Contributes to group effort	
B. *Teaches Others New Skills*	
C. *Serves Clients/Customers*—Works to satisfy customers' expectations	
D. *Exercises Leadership*—Communicates ideas to justify position, persuades and convinces others, responsibly challenges existing procedures and policies	
E. *Negotiates*—Works toward agreements involving exchange of resources, resolves divergent interests	
F. *Works with Diversity*—Works well with men and women from diverse backgrounds	

III. INFORMATION: Acquires and uses information   1–22

   A. *Acquires and Evaluates Information*

   B. *Organizes and Maintains Information*

   C. *Interprets and Communicates Information*

   D. *Uses Computers to Process Information*

IV. SYSTEMS: Understands complex interrelationships   4–22

   A. *Understands Systems*—Knows how social, organizational, and technological systems work and operates effectively with them

   B. *Monitors and Corrects Performance*—Distinguishes trends, predicts impacts on system operations, diagnoses deviations in systems' performance and corrects them

   C. *Improves or Designs Systems*—Suggests modifications to existing systems and develops new or alternative systems to improve performance

V. TECHNOLOGY: Works with a variety of technologies   4–22

   A. *Selects Technology*—Chooses procedures, tools, or equipment, including computers and related technologies

   B. *Applies Technology to Task*—Understands overall intent and proper procedures for setup and operation of equipment

   C. *Troubleshoots Equipment*—Prevents, identifies, or solves problems with equipment, including computers and other technologies

Curriculum Guide

Glencoe's *Medical Terminology—Language for Health Care* can be used for a one-semester or two-semester course. The anatomy and physiology sections of each chapter can either be read just for the terms or studied for the knowledge presented. Instructors who wish to cover anatomy and physiology only as it is necessary for understanding definitions can have students read for the key terms and use the vocabulary review sections to reinforce the terms, their pronunciations, and their definitions. Instructors who emphasize the underlying anatomy and physiology can have students study the structure and function sections in detail.

References and Resources

Glencoe's *Medical Terminology—Language for Health Care* uses Stedman's *Medical Dictionary*, 26th edition, as its standard for pronunciations. Many other references and resources including many original sources were used in the writing of this text.

Additional resources are available to instructors from the many health care organizations, the thousands of Websites on the Internet devoted to health issues, and the many federal and state agencies that service and oversee organizations that service the health care needs of the population.

Health-Related Organizations—Hotline Numbers

The toll-free telephone numbers of many organizations are available online (http://www. healthfinder.gov). The healthfinder site provides a directory of toll-free numbers of organizations listed by disease or medical information category. The list below is a small sample of numbers available. Many organizations will provide free brochures, newsletters, and other materials.

Subject	Organization	Toll-Free Number
AIDS	CDC National AIDS Clearinghouse	800 458-5231
Allergy	Asthma and Allergy Foundation of America	800 727-8462
Alzheimer's	Alzheimer's Association	800 272-3900
Arthritis	Arthritis Foundation	800 283-7800
Cancer	American Cancer Society	800 227-2345
Diabetes	American Diabetes Association	800 232-3472
Heart Disease	American Heart Association	800 242-8721
Hospice	National Hospice Organization	800 658-8898
Kidney	National Kidney Foundation	800 622-9010
Mental Health	National Alliance for the Mentally Ill	800 950-6264
Nutrition	American Dietetic Association	800 877-1600

Health-Related Websites

Note: This is a sample of some health-related Websites. Websites change frequently so these addresses cannot be guaranteed. However, it is usually possible to find a Website that has changed by going to one of the many search engines and searching the Web using some key terms from the name of the Website.

Alcoholics Anonymous: www.alcoholics-anonymous.org
American Association on Mental Retardation: www.aamr.org
American Cancer Society: www.cancer.org
American Dental Association: www.ada.org
American Diabetes Association: www.diabetes.org
American Heart Association: www.amhrt.org
American Lung Association: www.lungusa.org
American Psychological Association: www.apa.org
Arthritis Foundation: www.arthritis.org
Centers for Disease Control: www.cdc.gov
Food and Drug Administration: www.fda.gov
The Leukemia and Lymphoma Society: www.leukemia.org
National Cancer Institute: www.nci.nih.gov
National Osteoporosis Foundation: www.nof.org

Chapter 1 Learning Terminology

The chapter on learning terminology introduces the history of the formal language of medicine. In the process of discussing medical terminology development, the chapter introduces etymology, the formation of words, the spelling, pronunciation, and pluralizing of terms. Medical documentation and the legal and ethical issues relating to allied health professions are covered briefly.

Since Chapter 1 contains only introductory material, it does not include extensive exercises. It does test students' knowledge of the basic rules of pluralizing as well as of some of the elements of medical documentation.

If the medical terminology course has the time available, this chapter may be used for discussion purposes, particularly on legal and ethical issues as they relate to medical personnel.

1. **Creative Thinking**—Have each student or student group imagine a legal or ethical situation that might arise in a work situation. Students can then discuss the pros and cons of various ways of handling such situations.

2. **Practicing Pluralizing**—Have students read the rules for pluralizing terms and come up with as many medical term plurals as they can. (Self-study students and distance learners can use the index or any of the chapter reviews in the body system chapters to pick out words to pluralize.)

3. **Reinforcing Spelling**—With books closed, have students spell selected words that you read aloud to them from the index or body system chapter review lists. (Self-study students and distance learners should use the audiotapes or the CD-ROM, by covering the screen and listening to the audio only, to test themselves. They should write down the words as they listen and check their spelling against the text.)

4. **Using Medical Documents**—Choose a medical document from the section starting on page 91 of this Instructor's Manual. Ask students questions about the document to see if they comprehend the information. (Supply distance learners with a medical document and have them fill out as much as they can, providing information for an imaginary patient.)

5. **Learning Terms**—Have students watch a medically oriented television show and listen for at least three medical terms (preferably about human development). Write down the terms and their meanings.

6. **Newsworthy Notes**—Have each student bring in one newspaper article (or even an advertisement) or an Internet printout about legal or ethical medical issues. Students should discuss the article briefly in class.

Chapter 1:   Test of Pluralizing (25 Questions, 4 pts. each)

Give the plurals for the following terms. Where possible, give two different plurals.

1. carcinoma _____

2. frenulum _____

3. serum _____

4. psychosis _____

5. virus _____

6. septum _____

7. femur _____

8. kidney _____

9. tongue _____

10. urethra _____

11. ureter _____

12. malignancy _____

13. leukocyte _____

14. nucleus _____

15. reflex _____

16. tremor _____

17. venogram _____

18. suture _____

19. macula _____

20. thrombus _____

21. tricuspid _____

22. respiration _____

23. antibiotic _____

24. fungus _____

25. palate _____

Chapter 2 Building Medical Terms

Chapters 2 and 3 introduce the word parts that form many of the medical terms now in use. Chapter 2 introduces common prefixes, suffixes, and general combining forms that are used in medical terminology. These include the combining forms that are not specific to individual body systems (those combining forms are covered in Chapter 3).

In this chapter, students must begin the process of memorizing word parts that they will see in many terms. Once they learn the word parts, they will be able to understand many terms without having seen them earlier. The key to such memorization is repetition. There are a number of ways students can repeat the word parts without just reading them over and over again.

1. **Building Vocabulary**—Have each student gradually build a flash card collection for the prefixes, suffixes, and combining forms in this chapter. Since there are so many, you may want to have each student choose only those forms that seem unfamiliar to them. Alternatively, you may want to assign them a certain number of prefixes, suffixes, and combining forms to make flash cards for each day. Each flash card should show the prefix, suffix, or combining form on the front and have the definition and at least two examples on the back. See page viii of this manual for instructions.

2. **Using Resources**—Have each student or student group choose a health-related Website on the Internet. Ask them to find at least five terms that are based on a prefix, suffix, or combining form found in this chapter.

3. **Using Medical Documents**—Choose a medical document from the section starting on page 91 of this Instructor's Manual. Ask students to fill in terms that are made up of the word parts in this chapter. (Supply distance learners with a medical document and have them fill out as much as they can, providing terms made up of the word parts in this chapter.)

4. **Learning Terms**—Have students watch a medically oriented television show and listen for at least three medical terms (preferably made up of word parts found in this chapter). Write down the terms and their meanings.

5. **Newsworthy Notes**—Have each student bring in one newspaper article (or even an advertisement) or an Internet printout that includes terms made up of word parts found in this chapter.

Chapter 2: Word Building (20 questions—5 pts. each)

Using the following word parts, complete the word that best fits each definition given below. Word parts may be used more than once.

ambi-	bacteri(o)	lith(o)	-pathy
anti-	chrom(o)	-lytic	phot(o)
-algia	cyt(o)	mega	-plasty
-asthenia	-cyte	-megaly	-rrhea
aut(o)-	gyn(o)	path(o)	therm(o)

1. Nerve pain: neur _____ .

2. Bone repair: osteo _____ .

3. Study of disease: _____ logy.

4. Nerve weakness: neur _____ .

5. Abnormally enlarged head: _____ cephaly.

6. Enlarged heart: cardio _____ .

7. Dissolving of stones: _____ lytic.

8. Caused by bacteria: _____ genic.

9. Of both sides: _____ lateral.

10. Cell formed in lymph: lympho _____ .

11. Agent that kills cells: _____ cide.

12. Repair of the nose: rhino _____ .

13. Self-love: _____ philia.

14. Production of heat: _____ genesis.

15. Pigmented cell: _____ cyte.

16. Foot pain: pod _____ .

17. Female disease: _____ pathy.

18. Drug reducing bleeding: _____ hemorrhagic.

19. Sensitivity to light: _____ phobia.

20. Nasal discharge: rhino _____ .

Chapter 3 Body Structure

Chapter 3 introduces the medical terms that describe the elements of human body structure, including the planes of the body, the body cavities and the organs contained therein, and the combining forms that relate to individual body systems. (General word parts used in medical terminology are covered in Chapter 2.)

This chapter begins the study of the basics of human anatomy, starting with the overall body structure, the terms used to describe the planes of the body, and the body cavities. The material learned here sets the stage for learning the structure and function of each individual body system. In this chapter, students must continue the process of memorizing word parts that they will see in many terms. Once they learn the word parts, they will be able to understand many terms without having seen them earlier. The key to such memorization is repetition. There are a number of ways students can repeat the word parts without just reading them over and over again.

1. **Building Vocabulary**—Have each student gradually build a flash card collection for the combining forms in this chapter. Since there are so many, you may want to have each student choose only those forms that seem unfamiliar to them. Alternatively, you may want to assign them a certain number of combining forms to make flash cards for each day. Each flash card should show the combining form on the front and have the definition and at least two examples on the back. See page viii of this manual for instructions.

2. **Using Resources**—Have each student or student group choose a health-related Website on the Internet. Ask them to find at least five terms that are based on a combining form found in this chapter.

3. **Using Medical Documents**—Choose a medical document from the section starting on page 91 of this Instructor's Manual. Ask students to fill in terms that are made up of the word parts in this chapter or that describe the planes of the body or body positioning. (Supply distance learners with a medical document and have them fill out as much as they can, providing terms made up of the word parts in this chapter.)

4. **Learning Terms**—Have students watch a medically oriented television show and listen for at least three medical terms (preferably made up of word parts found in this chapter). Write down the terms and their meanings.

5. **Newsworthy Notes**—Have each student bring in one newspaper article (or even an advertisement) or an Internet printout that includes terms made up of word parts found in this chapter.

Chapter 3: Word-Building (20 questions—5 pts. each)

Using the following combining forms, complete the word that best fits the definition of each word relating to body structure listed below. Combining forms may be used more than once.

angi(o)	enter(o)	lip(o)	or(o)
aort(o)	gastr(o)	medull(o)	phleb(o)
arthr(o)	hidr(o)	my(o)	pneum(o)
cerebr(o)	kerat(o)	ophthalm(o)	somat(o)
crani(o)	laryng(o)	osteo	trache(o)

1. Stomach inflammation: _____ itis.

2. Swelling in subcutaneous fat: _____ edema.

3. Intestinal suture: _____ rrhaphy.

4. Body pain: _____ algia.

5. Joint disease: _____ pathy.

6. Vein incision: _____ tomy.

7. Sweat production: _____ osis.

8. Instrument for eye examination: _____ scope.

9. Blood vessel repair: _____ plasty.

10. Of the brain and spinal cord: _____ spinal.

11. Intentional bone fracture: _____ clasis.

12. Corneal disease: _____ pathy.

13. Of the mouth and face: _____ facial.

14. Removal of part of the lung: _____ resection.

15. Muscle tumor: _____ oma.

16. Inflammation of the main artery: _____ itis.

17. Incision into the larynx: _____ tomy.

18. Removal of marrow: _____ ectomy.

19. Softening of the skull: _____ malacia.

20. Surgical fixing of the intestine: _____ pexy.

Chapter 4 The Integumentary System

In addition to the general discussion of teaching by body systems in the introduction to this Instructor's Manual, the following suggestions provide specific class activities. For instructors involved in distance learning, you may want to assign some of these as self-directed student activities.

1. **Building Vocabulary**—Have each student make a flash card for each combining form on pages 78–79 of the textbook. Each flash card should show the combining form on the front and have the definition and at least two examples on the back. See page viii of this manual for instructions.

2. **Using Resources**—Have each student or student group choose one part of the integumentary system. Instruct them to use the library and the Internet to list functions of and potential diseases that may occur in that part. Have them report to the class if possible.

3. **Creative Thinking**—Using the form below, have students choose an integumentary disease and make up a fictional series medical chart for a person with that disease. Have them list symptoms, potential treatments, and outlook.

Patient Name _____ Date _____

ID # _____ Date of Birth _____ Insurance carrier _____

Date   Time of Visit   Notes

_____

_____

_____

_____

_____

4. **Practicing Pronunciation**—Have students read the Chapter Review list out loud either together or sequentially. Stop and correct any mistakes in pronunciation. (Self-study students and distance learners can refer to the audiotapes and CD-ROM and compare their pronunciations to the ones given.)

5. **Reinforcing Spelling**—With books closed, have students spell selected words that you read aloud to them from the Chapter Review list. Have any student who spells a word incorrectly write it on the blackboard or a piece of paper 10 times. (Self-study students and distance learners should use the audiotapes or the CD-ROM, by covering the screen and listening to the audio only, to test themselves. They should write down the words as they listen and check their spelling against the text.)

6. **Learning the Roots**—Read aloud integumentary system words that are made up of word parts. Have students name the parts and define the words. (Self-study students and distance learners should use the Chapter Review lists to pick out words that can be divided into word parts. They should write the word parts and check them in the chapter itself or in a medical dictionary.)

7. **Using Medical Documents**—Choose a medical document from the section starting on page 91 of this Instructor's Manual. Ask students questions about the document to see if they comprehend the information. (Supply distance learners with a medical document and have them fill out as much as they can, providing information for a person with an integumentary system disease.)

8. **Learning Terms**—Have students watch a medically oriented television show and listen for at least three medical terms (preferably about the integumentary system). Write down the terms and their meanings.

9. **Building a Case Study**—As an end-of-chapter project, have the class build a case study. They can start with a dermatologist and one or two patients with integumentary system pathologies. Have them build part of each patient's file showing doctor's notes, tests requested, results, and treatments. Each student may be assigned a role in the development of the case study. (Self-study students or distance learners can use the Internet to write a short part of a case study about a patient with a particular disease.)

10. **Newsworthy Notes**—Have each student bring in one newspaper article (or even an advertisement) or an Internet printout about integumentary health, particularly as it relates to sun exposure. Students should discuss the article briefly in class.

Chapter 4: Word-Building (20 questions—5 pts. each)

Using the following combining forms, complete the word that best fits the definition of each word relating to the integumentary system listed below. Combining forms may be used more than once.

adip(o)	ichthy(o)	myc(o)	steat(o)
dermat(o)	kerat(o)	onych(o)	trich(o)
derm(o)	lip(o)	pil(o)	xanth(o)
hidr(o)	melan(o)	seb(o)	xer(o)

1. Skin contraction: _____ stenosis.

2. Study of fungi: _____ logy.

3. Abnormal nail softness: _____ malacia.

4. Skin hemorrhage: _____ rrhea.

5. Deficiency of fats: _____ penia.

6. Inflammation of fatty tissue: _____ itis.

7. Yellowish skin: _____ derma.

8. Fat cell: _____ cyte.

9. Marbled skin: _____ leukoderma.

10. Dry skin: _____ osis.

11. Formation of a horny layer: _____ plasia.

12. Nail biting: _____ phagia.

13. Scraping procedure used on the skin: _____ abrasion.

14. Excessive lip dryness: _____ chilia.

15. Fish-shaped: _____ oid.

16. Yellow skin nodule: _____ oma.

17. Hair examination: _____ scopy.

18. Overactivity of the sebaceous glands: _____ rrhea.

19. Fungal condition: _____ osis.

20. Scaling of the skin: _____ osis.

```
d  e  c  u  b  i  t  u  s  o  u  c  u  r  r  e  t  t  a  g  e
e  e  o  r  p  m  q  x  e  n  o  g  r  a  f  t  u  s  k  d  o
r  u  b  i  l  l  u  o  t  l  b  t  g  h  i  k  c  h  p  e  d
m  p  u  r  p  u  r  a  d  o  u  r  d  h  a  c  o  m  u  r  i
a  e  r  o  i  o  d  i  s  p  s  c  l  e  r  o  d  e  r  m  a
t  u  n  r  l  d  r  m  o  c  c  h  u  r  r  m  o  d  t  i  b
i  n  d  i  o  v  e  e  r  m  h  i  n  p  h  e  m  o  i  s  s
t  r  o  l  n  d  i  m  e  l  i  g  u  e  l  d  s  n  c  t  c
i  s  t  g  i  n  i  g  e  i  c  r  l  s  o  o  c  o  a  u  e
s  w  u  l  d  a  m  h  u  n  k  o  a  c  n  e  a  r  r  p  s
s  w  l  a  a  l  r  t  r  d  t  u  l  c  r  a  b  m  i  l  s
w  e  e  t  l  e  u  k  o  d  e  r  m  a  l  m  i  n  a  e  e
n  o  d  a  l  g  r  a  m  u  s  t  h  a  l  l  e  p  e  x  b
o  n  y  c  t  g  l  a  n  d  t  r  i  s  c  l  s  a  c  c  u
i  m  p  e  t  i  g  o  s  c  h  i  c  k  h  u  l  y  i  o  m
t  i  o  n  y  h  o  i  s  e  s  s  i  l  e  t  l  m  s  r  l
a  t  j  n  m  y  s  d  a  m  r  t  d  e  p  a  r  e  i  t  t
i  a  i  l  n  o  t  i  r  i  n  g  w  o  r  m  o  l  m  i  s
r  r  l  u  p  y  i  t  c  i  s  l  e  o  i  d  p  a  r  o  u
o  o  n  a  u  r  c  h  o  p  a  t  h  y  r  l  o  n  e  n  l
c  p  k  e  l  o  i  d  m  i  m  o  u  s  t  h  r  o  d  a  p
x  e  p  o  r  m  i  l  a  l  l  w  a  l  o  p  e  c  i  a  o
e  x  o  c  r  i  n  e  g  l  d  s  n  a  i  p  r  y  p  j  o
s  t  l  r  e  l  a  r  m  p  e  d  i  c  u  l  a  t  e  k  d
s  o  u  u  l  o  i  d  y  u  a  t  o  y  u  l  c  e  r  l  e
e  i  c  s  k  i  l  l  d  e  r  m  a  s  t  o  p  l  k  i  r
s  d  e  t  m  d  o  n  y  c  h  o  p  a  t  h  y  r  m  d  m
d  e  r  t  i  p  n  i  d  a  l  p  o  p  t  y  q  u  i  t  s
```

Figure 4.1. Word Find for Chapter 4. Circle at least 20 words in this puzzle that are listed in the Chapter Review section of the textbook. Answers are on page 87 of this Instructor's Manual.

Chapter 5 The Musculoskeletal System

Teaching Suggestions

In addition to the general discussion of teaching by body systems in the introduction to this Instructor's Manual, the following suggestions provide specific class activities. For instructors involved in distance learning, you may want to assign some of these as self-directed student activities.

1. **Building Vocabulary**—Have each student make a flash card for each combining form on pages 126–129 of the textbook. Each flash card should show the combining form on the front and have the definition and at least two examples on the back. See page viii of this manual for instructions.

2. **Using Resources**—Have each student or student group choose one part of the musculoskeletal system. Instruct them to use the library and the Internet to list functions of and potential diseases that may occur in that part. Have them report to the class if possible.

3. **Creative Thinking**—Using the HCFA form on page 92, have students choose a musculoskeletal disease and make up a fictional HCFA form to be submitted for a person with that disease.

4. **Practicing Pronunciation**—Have students read the Chapter Review list out loud either together or sequentially. Stop and correct any mistakes in pronunciation. (Self-study students and distance learners can refer to the audiotapes and CD-ROM and compare their pronunciations to the ones given.)

5. **Reinforcing Spelling**—With books closed, have students spell selected words that you read aloud to them from the Chapter Review list. Have any student who spells a word incorrectly write it on the blackboard or a piece of paper 10 times. (Self-study students and distance learners should use the audiotapes or the CD-ROM, by covering the screen and listening to the audio only, to test themselves. They should write down the words as they listen and check their spelling against the text.)

6. **Learning the Roots**—Read aloud musculoskeletal system words that are made up of word parts. Have students name the parts and define the words. (Self-study students and distance learners should use the Chapter Review lists to pick out words that can be divided into word parts. They should write the word parts and check them in the chapter itself or in a medical dictionary.)

7. **Using Medical Documents**—Choose a medical document from the section starting on page 91 of this Instructor's Manual. Ask students questions about the document to see if they comprehend the information. (Supply distance learners with a medical document and have them fill out as much as they can, providing information for a person with a musculoskeletal system disease.)

8. **Learning Terms**—Have students watch a medically oriented television show and listen for at least three medical terms (preferably about the musculoskeletal system). Write down the terms and their meanings.

9. **Building a Case Study**—As an end-of-chapter project, have the class build a case study. They can start with a patient with osteoporosis. Give some medical history that discusses possible causes of the disease. Discuss the course of the disease, treatments, tests requested, and results. Each student may be assigned a role in the development of the case study. (Self-study students or distance learners can use the Internet to write a short part of a case study about a patient with osteoporosis.)

10. **Newsworthy Notes**—Have each student bring in one newspaper article (or even an advertisement) or an Internet printout about musculoskeletal health, particularly as it relates to the intake of calcium. Students should discuss the article briefly in class.

Chapter 5:   Word-Building (20 questions—5 pts. each)

Using the following combining forms, complete the word that best fits the definition of each word relating to the musculoskeletal system listed below. Combining forms may be used more than once.

acetabul(o)	cost(o)	lamin(o)	radi(o)
brachi(o)	dactyl(o)	lumb(o)	scapul(o)
burs(o)	femor(o)	myel(o)	stern(o)
calci(o)	fibr(o)	patell(o)	synov(o)
cervic(o)	kyph(o)	ped(i)	uln(o)

1. Formation of bone marrow tissue: _____ poiesis.

2. Relating to the arm and head: _____ cephalic.

3. Toward the ulna: _____ ad.

4. Repair of part of the hip: _____ plasty.

5. Condition with insufficient calcium: _____ penia.

6. Inflammation of a lamina: _____ itis.

7. Surgical fixing of the scapula: _____ pexy.

8. Cyst with fibrous tissue: _____ cyst.

9. Patella pain: _____ algia.

10. Of the sternum and pericardium: _____ pericardial.

11. Swelling of the finger: _____ edema.

12. Of the lumbar vertebrae and the ribs: _____ costal.

13. Relating to the neck and arm: _____ brachial.

14. Of the radius and humerus: _____ humeral.

15. Brace used for the spine: _____ tone.

16. Care of the feet: _____ cure.

17. Inflammation of the synovial membrane: _____ itis.

18. Spasm of the fingers: _____ spasm.

19. Of the upper ribs: _____ superior.

20. Neck pain: _____ dynia.

Figure 5.1. Crossword for Chapter 5. Answers are on page 88 of this Instructor's Manual.

CLUES

ACROSS

1. Spur
3. Bone pain
5. Inflammation of the joints
8. Long thigh bone
10. Patella
11. _____ valgus
13. Device to measure angle of motion
15. Part of the scapula
17. Type of fracture
19. Involuntary movement
22. Bone _____
24. Physician who gives manipulative treatment
25. Lower leg bone
27. Portion of the hip bone
29. _____ fluid
31. Joining of two bone parts
34. Ring of bone at the base of the trunk
36. Muscle tumor
37. Joint repair

DOWN

1. Collar bone
2. _____ disk
3. Incision into bone
4. Depression in the hip bone
6. Back portion of the foot
7. Bony structure
9. Stiffening
12. Vitamin D deficiency
14. Imaging of a joint
16. Intentional breaking of a bone
18. Bone formed in a tendon
20. Artificial device
21. Section of long bone
23. First cervical vertebra
26. Joining place of two bones
28. Removal of a bursa
30. Bony segments of the spine
32. _____ acid test
33. Combining form meaning rod-shaped
35. Nasal septum bone

Chapter 6 The Cardiovascular System

Teaching Suggestions

In addition to the general discussion of teaching by body systems in the introduction to this Instructor's Manual, the following suggestions provide specific class activities. For instructors involved in distance learning, you may want to assign some of these as self-directed student activities.

1. **Building Vocabulary**—Have each student make a flash card for each combining form on pages 178–179 of the textbook. Each flash card should show the combining form on the front and have the definition and at least two examples on the back. See page viii of this manual for instructions.

2. **Using Resources**—Have each student or student group choose one part of the cardiovascular system. Instruct them to use the library and the Internet to list functions of and potential diseases that may occur in that part. Have them report to the class if possible.

3. **Creative Thinking**—Using the form below, have students choose a cardiovascular disease and make up a fictional, "personal" medical history. Discuss their histories in class with an emphasis on how they might have taken steps earlier to change their medical history.

Patient Name _____   Diagnosis _____

Family History:

Family Member _____; Relationship _____; Diseases _____

Family Member _____; Relationship _____; Diseases _____

Family Member _____; Relationship _____; Diseases _____

Family Member _____; Relationship _____; Diseases _____

Family Member _____; Relationship _____; Diseases _____

Family Member _____; Relationship _____; Diseases _____

Risk Factors:

Smoking _____ If yes, how long _____

Obesity _____ If yes, percentage of overweight _____

Stress _____ If yes, choose a number to indicate extent (10 high; 1 low) _____

High overall cholesterol _____ Number _____

Ratio of HDL to LDL _____

Diabetes _____ If yes, how long _____

High blood pressure _____ If yes, numbers _____

Symptoms:

List symptoms that you feel are related to your cardiovascular illness.

_____

_____

4. **Practicing Pronunciation**—Have students read the Chapter Review list out loud either together or sequentially. Stop and correct any mistakes in pronunciation. (Self-study students and distance learners can refer to the audiotapes and CD-ROM and compare their pronunciations to the ones given.)

5. **Reinforcing Spelling**—With books closed, have students spell selected words that you read aloud to them from the Chapter Review list. Have any student who spells a word incorrectly write it on the blackboard or a piece of paper 10 times. (Self-study students and distance learners should use the audiotapes or the CD-ROM, by covering the screen and listening to the audio only, to test themselves. They should write down the words as they listen and check their spelling against the text.)

6. **Learning the Roots**—Read aloud cardiovascular system words that are made up of word parts. Have students name the parts and define the words. (Self-study students and distance learners should use the Chapter Review lists to pick out words that can be divided into word parts. They should write the word parts and check them in the chapter itself or in a medical dictionary.)

7. **Using Medical Documents**—Choose a medical document from the section starting on page 91 of this Instructor's Manual. Ask students questions about the document to see if they comprehend the information. (Supply distance learners with a medical document and have them fill out as much as they can, providing information for a person with a cardiovascular system disease.)

8. **Learning Terms**—Have students watch a medically oriented television show and listen for at least three medical terms (preferably about the cardiovascular system). Write down the terms and their meanings.

9. **Building a Case Study**—As an end-of-chapter project, have the class build a case study. They can start with a patient with cardiovascular disease. Give some medical history that discusses possible causes of the disease. Discuss the course of the disease, treatments, tests requested, and results. Each student may be assigned a role in the development of the case study. (Self-study students or distance learners can use the Internet to write a short part of a case study about a patient with cardiovascular disease.)

10. **Newsworthy Notes**—Have each student bring in one newspaper article (or even an advertisement) or an Internet printout about cardiovascular health, particularly as it relates to prevention. Students should discuss the article briefly in class.

Chapter 6: Word-Building (20 questions—5 pts. each)

Using the following combining forms, complete the word that best fits the definition of each word relating to the cardiovascular system listed below. Combining forms may be used more than once.

angi(o)	cardi(o)	thromb(o)
aort(o)	hemangi(o)	vas(o)
arteri(o)	pericardi(o)	ven(o)
ather(o)	phleb(o)	
atri(o)	sphygm(o)	

1. Dissolving of a blood clot: _____ lysis.

2. Inflammation of the pericardium: _____ itis.

3. Blood clot in the heart: _____ thrombus.

4. Formation of atheromas: _____ genesis.

5. Heart paralysis: _____ plegia.

6. Hardening of the arteries: _____ sclerosis.

7. Hardening of the veins: _____ sclerosis.

8. Imaging of the aorta: _____ graphy.

9. Feeling the pulse: _____ palpation.

10. Suture of the pericardium: _____ rrhaphy.

11. Study of blood vessels: _____ logy.

12. Disease of the arteries: _____ pathy.

13. Resembling blood vessels: _____ oid.

14. Rupture in the heart: _____ rrhexis.

15. Agent that narrows blood vessels: _____ constrictor.

16. Presence of a blood clot: _____ osis.

17. Incision into the heart: _____ tomy.

18. Throbbing of an artery: _____ palmus.

19. Abnormally enlarged atrium: _____ megaly.

20. Aortal narrowing: _____ stenosis.

Figure 6.1. Crossword for Chapter 6. Answers are on page 88 of this Instructor's Manual.

CLUES

ACROSS

1. Vein inflammation
3. Carry oxygenated blood
4. Fatty substance
7. One unit of pulse
9. Electrocardiogram
11. Combining form for muscle
13. _____maker
14. Tiny blood vessel
15. Partition between heart chambers
17. Bishop's hat valve
18. Heart sound heard on auscultation
19. Localized blood insufficiency
23. Largest artery
24. _____ arteriosus
25. Incision into a valve
26. _____ inhibitor
28. Frictional sound heard on auscultation
29. Upper right heart chamber
31. Medication that dilates veins
32. Chest pain
33. High blood pressure

DOWN

1. Rhythmical expansion and contraction
2. Contraction phase of blood pressure
3. Of the atrium
5. Channel inside artery
6. Able to lower cholesterol
8. Abnormally fast heart rate
10. Bluish coloration
12. Place where blood enters the heart from systemic circulation
16. Muscular layer of heart tissue
18. Bicuspid valve
20. Muscular organ that circulates blood
21. Abnormally slow heart rate
22. Closing of a blood vessel
27. Implanted tissue
28. Pace of heart beat
30. _____ blood pressure

Chapter 7 The Respiratory System

In addition to the general discussion of teaching by body systems in the introduction to this Instructor's Manual, the following suggestions provide specific class activities. For instructors involved in distance learning, you may want to assign some of these as self-directed student activities.

1. **Building Vocabulary**—Have each student make a flash card for each combining form on pages 233–235 of the textbook. Each flash card should show the combining form on the front and have the definition and at least two examples on the back. See page viii of this manual for instructions.

2. **Using Resources**—Have each student or student group choose one part of the respiratory system. Instruct them to use the library and the Internet to list functions of and potential diseases that may occur in that part. Have them report to the class if possible.

3. **Creative Thinking**—Using the form below, have students choose a respiratory disease and make up a fictional series medical chart for a person with that disease. Have them list symptoms, potential treatments, and outlook.

Patient Name _____ Date _____

ID # _____ Date of Birth _____ Insurance carrier _____

Date   Time of Visit   Notes

_____

_____

_____

_____

_____

_____

4. **Practicing Pronunciation**—Have students read the Chapter Review list out loud either together or sequentially. Stop and correct any mistakes in pronunciation. (Self-study students and distance learners can refer to the audiotapes and CD-ROM and compare their pronunciations to the ones given.)

5. **Reinforcing Spelling**—With books closed, have students spell selected words that you read aloud to them from the Chapter Review list. Have any student who spells a word incorrectly write it on the blackboard or a piece of paper 10 times. (Self-study students and distance learners should use the audiotapes or the CD-ROM, by covering the screen and listening to the audio only, to test themselves. They should write down the words as they listen and check their spelling against the text.)

6. **Learning the Roots**—Read aloud respiratory words that are made up of word parts. Have students name the parts and define the words. (Self-study students and distance learners should use the Chapter Review lists to pick out words that can be divided into word parts. They should write the word parts and check them in the chapter itself or in a medical dictionary.)

7. **Using Medical Documents**—Choose a medical document from the section starting on page 91 of this Instructor's Manual. Ask students questions about the document to see if they comprehend the information. (Supply distance learners with a medical document and have them fill out as much as they can, providing information for a person with a respiratory disease.)

8. **Learning Terms**—Have students watch a medically oriented television show and listen for at least three medical terms (preferably about the respiratory system). Write down the terms and their meanings.

9. **Building a Case Study**—As an end-of-chapter project, have the class build a case study. They can start with an otorhinolaryngologist and one or two patients with respiratory pathologies. Have them build part of each patient's file showing doctor's notes, tests requested, results, and treatments. Each student may be assigned a role in the development of the case study. (Self-study students or distance learners can use the Internet to write a short part of a case study about a patient with a particular disease.)

10. **Newsworthy Notes**—Have each student bring in one newspaper article (or even an advertisement) or an Internet printout about respiratory health. Students should discuss the article briefly in class.

Figure 7.1. Crossword for Chapter 7. Answers are on page 88 of this Instructor's Manual.

CLUES

ACROSS

1. External breathing structure
3. Membrane on the outside of the lungs
5. _____ sample
7. Hiccuping
9. Vibrations produce sound
12. Bronchial narrowing condition
14. Popping sounds
17. Combining form for lung
18. Windpipe
21. Organ of voice production
23. Oxygen deficiency
24. Acute alveolar infection
25. Whistling sound on inspiration
27. Abnormally deep breathing
30. Combining form for mouth
33. Combining form for breath
35. Middle section of the right lung
36. Repair of a nasal septum

DOWN

1. Inflammation of the nose and pharynx
2. Paranasal cavity
3. Of the lung
4. Air sacs in the lungs
5. Lung condition
6. Rare type of lung cancer
8. High-pitched respiratory sound
10. Hairlike extensions
11. Division of the pharynx
13. Procedure to prevent choking
15. Organ of respiration
16. Abnormally slow breathing
19. Inflammation of the pleura
20. To breathe out
22. Exhalation
25. Trachea
26. Lymphoid tissue in the nasopharynx
27. Midsection of the lung
28. Of the thorax
29. One section of the lung
31. Pharynx
32. Peak _____
34. Crackles

Name _____ Date _____

Chapter 7:   Word-Building (20 questions—5 pts. each)

Using the following combining forms, complete the word that best fits the definition of each word relating to the respiratory system listed below. Combining forms may be used more than once.

adenoid(o)	epiglott(o)	or(o)	pneum(o)
alveol(o)	laryng(o)	ox(o)	spir(o)
bronchi(o)	lob(o)	phon(o)	steth(o)
bronch(o)	mediastin(o)	phren(o)	thorac(o)
capn(o)	nas(o)	pleur(o)	trache(o)

1. Of the epiglottis: _____ ic.

2. Destruction of the alveolus: _____ clasia.

3. Incision into a lobe: _____ tomy.

4. Abnormal voice production: _____ asthenia.

5. Inflammation of the bronchus: _____ itis.

6. Device for measuring respiration: _____ graph.

7. Washing out of the pleura: _____ clysis.

8. Inflammation of the nose and sinuses: _____ sinusitis.

9. Incision into the chest wall: _____ tomy.

10. Removal of the adenoids: _____ ectomy.

11. Paralysis of the diaphragm: _____ plegia.

12. Inflammation of the larynx and trachea: _____ tracheitis.

13. Compound of oxygen: _____ ide.

14. Excessive bronchial mucus: _____ rrhea.

15. Recording of carbon dioxide: _____ gram.

16. Device for examining the mediastinum: _____ scope.

17. Inflammation of a lobe: _____ itis.

18. Narrowing of the bronchial tube: _____ stenosis.

19. Tracheal hemorrhage: _____ rrhagia.

20. Removal of the larynx: _____ ectomy.

Chapter 8 The Nervous System

Teaching Suggestions

In addition to the general discussion of teaching by body systems in the introduction to this Instructor's Manual, the following suggestions provide specific class activities. For instructors involved in distance learning, you may want to assign some of these as self-directed student activities.

1. **Building Vocabulary**—Have each student make a flash card for each combining form on pages 281–282 of the textbook. Each flash card should show the combining form on the front and have the definition and at least two examples on the back. See page viii of this manual for instructions.

2. **Using Resources**—Have each student or student group choose one part of the nervous system. Instruct them to use the library and the Internet to list functions of and potential diseases that may occur in that part. Have them report to the class if possible.

3. **Creative Thinking**—Using the form below, have students choose a nervous system disease and make up a daily chart of a nurse's rounds on a hospital ward that specializes in such diseases. Have them list symptoms, how the nurse helped the patients, and the patient's outlook.

Nurse _____ Date _____

Ward Number _____ Time of Rounds _____

Date   Patient   Notes

_____

_____

_____

_____

_____

_____

4. **Practicing Pronunciation**—Have students read the Chapter Review list out loud either together or sequentially. Stop and correct any mistakes in pronunciation. (Self-study students and distance learners can refer to the audiotapes and CD-ROM and compare their pronunciations to the ones given.)

5. **Reinforcing Spelling**—With books closed, have students spell selected words that you read aloud to them from the Chapter Review list. Have any student who spells a word incorrectly write it on the blackboard or a piece of paper 10 times. (Self-study students and distance learners should use the audiotapes or the CD-ROM, by covering the screen and listening to the audio only, to test themselves. They should write down the words as they listen and check their spelling against the text.)

6. **Learning the Roots**—Read aloud nervous system words that are made up of word parts. Have students name the parts and define the words. (Self-study students and distance learners should use the Chapter Review lists to pick out words that can be divided into word parts. They should write the word parts and check them in the chapter itself or in a medical dictionary.)

7. **Using Medical Documents**—Choose a medical document from the section starting on page 91 of this Instructor's Manual. Ask students questions about the document to see if they comprehend the information. (Supply distance learners with a medical document and have them fill out as much as they can providing information for a person with a nervous system disease.)

8. **Learning Terms**—Have students watch a medically oriented television show and listen for at least three medical terms (preferably about the nervous system). Write down the terms and their meanings.

9. **Building a Case Study**—As an end-of-chapter project, have the class build a case study. They can start with a psychiatrist and one or two patients with nervous system pathologies. Have them build part of each patient's file showing doctor's notes, tests requested, results, and treatments. Each student may be assigned a role in the development of the case study. (Self-study students or distance learners can use the Internet to write a short part of a case study about a patient with a particular disease.)

10. **Newsworthy Notes**—Have each student bring in one newspaper article (or even an advertisement) or an Internet printout about nervous system health. Students should discuss the article briefly in class.

Chapter 8:   Word-Building (20 questions — 5 pts. each)

Using the following combining forms, complete the word that best fits the definition of each word relating to the nervous system listed below. Combining forms may be used more than once.

cerebell(o)	gli(o)	thalam(o)
cerebr(o)	mening(o)	vag(o)
crani(o)	myel(o)	ventricul(o)
encephal(o)	neur(o)	
gangli(o)	spin(o)	

1. Of the blood supply in the brain: _____*cerebrovascular*_____ vascular.

2. Early neural cell: _____*glioblast*_____ blast.

3. Repair of the skull: _____*cranioplasty*_____ plasty.

4. Hardening of the brain: _____*encephalo*_____ sclerosis.

5. Inflammation of the meninges, brain, and spinal cord: _____*meningo*_____ encephalomyelitis.

6. Inflammation of the cerebellum: _____*cerebelitis*_____ itis.

7. Of the thalamus and cerebral cortex: _____*thalamo*_____ cortical.

8. Nerve pain: _____*neur*_____ algia.

9. Dissolving of a ganglion: _____*ganglio*_____ lysis.

10. Inflammation of the brain and spinal cord: _____*encephalo*_____ myelitis.

11. Opening in a ventricle: _____*ventriculo*_____ stomy.

12. Of the cerebrum and spinal cord: _____*cerebro*_____ spinal.

13. Attracted to the vagus nerve: _____*vago*_____ tropic.

14. Study of drugs that affect nerves: _____*neuro*_____ pharmacology.

15. Instrument for measuring the skull: _____*crani*_____ meter.

16. Mimicking the vagus nerve: _____*vago*_____ mimetic.

17. Hemorrhage from the meninges: _____*meningo*_____ rrhagia.

18. Incision into the cerebrum: _____*cerebro*_____ tomy.

19. Nervous system surgery: _____*neuro*_____ surgery.

20. Shaped like a ganglion: _____*gangli*_____ form.

```
p o n s a s d t y n e r u o n i o p o l c
y r e e a r v e m a r t l o e t o m a o e
r f r i u p l a s y t u i o r l p o m h r
o e v e t r i n s e d a t i v e r t n e e
g r o l o b o t o m y o g r e v o r e r b
e e t e n t h t h a l a m u s e i u s f e
n g u n o r t e r c r e e n c r u j i v l
i y j g m t h p i a m a t e r y y m a g l
c r a n i a l t h m n r e r v u t i n b u
m u y i c h o l l e s s i u o i s o g h m
a s n o m n i c i n o n m j t o i l i j a
n i g o p h i o m p a r k i n s o n s m n
v e i y o u n n t o n v e g t i u e t o g
e s h i n g l e s r o e a o m t a r e o a
s t r e p t o u r e t t e i n r e v r p i
n e r v y t b r a i n c e f f e r r e n t
e r g i m j e o n m i c i c i i n o m t e
y e r t y b c s h r t s t t h r o m b u s
c o r p u s t u s s s y r n e v u y o m c
m t h a l a o r a u m y e u s h r o l n i
o a a l k y m g r t h a n g e r t o u p a
a x o n e t y e r v a n g c o r m s s l t
n y c t o l t o m y a x u t o m y t e e i
m y o m s p i n a b i f i d a p e r v n c
f e r a l z h e i m e r s a r v e r e o a
p a r a s y m p a t h e t i c v e y r k t
e u r o g l c o n c u s s i o n i r v i e
a s t a s t r o c y t o m a r e t y o n r
```

Figure 8.1. Word Find for Chapter 8. Circle at least 20 words in this puzzle that are listed in the Chapter 8 Review section of the textbook. Answers are on page 88 of this Instructor's Manual.

Chapter 9 The Urinary System

Teaching Suggestions

In addition to the general discussion of teaching by body systems in the introduction to this Instructor's Manual, the following suggestions provide specific class activities. For instructors involved in distance learning, you may want to assign some of these as self-directed student activities.

1. **Building Vocabulary**—Have each student make a flash card for each combining form on page 317 of the textbook. Each flash card should show the combining form on the front and have the definition and at least two examples on the back. See page viii of this manual for instructions.

2. **Using Resources**—Have each student or student group choose one part of the urinary system. Instruct them to use the library and the Internet to list functions of and potential diseases that may occur in that part. Have them report to the class if possible.

3. **Creative Thinking**—Using the form below, have students make up a schedule for a urologist's day of patient and hospital work. Have them list patients, procedures, approximate time allowed, and any special notes.

Date _____

Hospital Rounds hours: _____

Time	Patient	Notes

Office hours: _____

Time	Patient	Notes

_____

_____

_____

4. **Practicing Pronunciation**—Have students read the Chapter Review list out loud either together or sequentially. Stop and correct any mistakes in pronunciation. (Self-study students and distance learners can refer to the audiotapes and CD-ROM and compare their pronunciations to the ones given.)

5. **Reinforcing Spelling**—With books closed, have students spell selected words that you read aloud to them from the Chapter Review list. Have any student who spells a word incorrectly write it on the blackboard or a piece of paper 10 times. (Self-study students and distance learners should use the audiotapes or the CD-ROM, by covering the screen and listening to the audio only, to test themselves. They should write down the words as they listen and check their spelling against the text.)

6. **Learning the Roots**—Read aloud urinary system words that are made up of word parts. Have students name the parts and define the words. (Self-study students and distance learners should use the Chapter Review lists to pick out words that can be divided into word parts. They should write the word parts and check them in the chapter itself or in a medical dictionary.)

7. **Using Medical Documents**—Choose a medical document from the section starting on page 91 of this Instructor's Manual. Ask students questions about the document to see if they comprehend the information. (Supply distance learners with a medical document and have them fill out as much as they can, providing information for a person with a urinary system disease.)

8. **Learning Terms**—Have students watch a medically oriented television show and listen for at least three medical terms (preferably about the urinary system). Write down the terms and their meanings.

9. **Building a Case Study**—As an end-of-chapter project, have the class build a case study. They can start with a patient with a urinary system pathology. Have them each build a part of the patient's file showing doctor's notes about the initial visits, tests requested, results, and treatments. Each student may be assigned a role in the development of the case study. (Self-study students or distance learners can use the Internet to write a short part of a case study about a patient with a particular disease.)

10. **Newsworthy Notes**—Have each student bring in one newspaper article (or even an advertisement) or an Internet printout about urinary system health. Students should discuss the article briefly in class.

Chapter 9: Word-Building (20 questions—5 pts. each)

Using the following combining forms, complete the word that best fits the definition of each word relating to the urinary system listed below. Combining forms may be used more than once.

cali(o)	nephr(o)	urin(o)
calic(o)	pyel(o)	ureter(o)
cyst(o)	reno	urethr(o)
glomerul(o)	trigon(o)	vesic(o)
meato	ur(o)	

1. Glomerular disease: _____glomerulo_____ pathy.

2. Inflammation of the urinary bladder: _____cyst_____ itis.

3. Kidney enlargement: _____nephro_____ megaly.

4. Removal of a bladder stone: _____cysto_____ lithotomy.

5. Instrument for inspecting the urethral passageway: _____cysto meato_____ scope.

6. Excessive urea in the blood: _____ur_____ emia.

7. Repair of a calyx: _____calico_____ plasty.

8. Narrowing of the urethra: _____urethro_____ stenosis.

9. Kidney tumor: _____nephr_____ oma.

10. Hernia of the urinary bladder: _____cysto_____ cele.

11. Study and treatment of the urinary system: _____uro_____ logy.

12. Repair of the meatus: _____meato_____ plasty.

13. Bladder suture: _____cysto_____ rrhaphy.

14. Incision into the calyx: _____cali_____ otomy.

15. Of the kidneys and stomach: _____reno_____ gastric.

16. Fluoroscopic examination of the renal pelvis: _____pyelo_____ fluoroscopy.

17. Inflammation of the bladder and urether: _____cysto_____ urethritis.

18. Kidney condition: _____nephr_____ osis.

19. Suture of the meatus: _____meato_____ rrhaphy.

20. Inflammation of the glomeruli of the kidney: _____glomerulo_____ nephritis.

```
n o c t u r i a r e c a t h e t e r r u u
e u l r u r t h n e c t o m y p r e u r r
p r u i l k m i n d w e l l i n g i t i i
h e t g g i r e r s i c r e a t i n e c n
r t e o r u r o l o g y s n i m o e r t a
o h m n u r r l i u s s s u e r e t h i l
l r n e h e e i k r o t a r e n o d r u y
i e e o i t s g a e r o m e g r a m e m s
t t p r o h i u d t h c y s t o l i t h i
h h h o l r s r n e t e l i g u r i a m s
o r r s u a a t e r r l u s t o p l i u r
t o o t m l i m y h u e n u r m e s i d e
o u s u r e t h r o t o m y l e m k t i r
m y i o m f i l t r a t i o n a t e r u h
y s s p e c i f i c g r a v i t y t u r e
a m c y s o y o p e x y m g l u c o s e m
l e t e r u h l i a n u r e s s i n o t a
a c a l y x y e x t h e m i a l y e p i t
z n s i c i c y s t i t i s t i c p y c u
o e e t y c o n i b l a d d e r t r o u r
r n s i s a r e s l u d d e r u r o r r i
e i e s o l t n u a m e d u l l a s r e a
t t r a t r e s i a d k i d n e y t h y i
e n u l i t x y l r e t h r a u y a e h a
r o n d i a l y s i s f i l t r a t i o n
n c p i u l m o n a r y v a r d i e a r t
h n o d y s u r i a z o t e m i a r s i o
u i a c a l i c x c y s t o s c o p y a n
```

Figure 9.1. Word Find for Chapter 9. Circle at least 20 words in this puzzle that are listed in the Chapter 9 Review section of the textbook. Answers are on page 89 of this Instructor's Manual.

Chapter 10 The Female Reproductive System

Teaching Suggestions

In addition to the general discussion of teaching by body systems in the introduction to this Instructor's Manual, the following suggestions provide specific class activities. For instructors involved in distance learning, you may want to assign some of these as self-directed student activities.

1. **Building Vocabulary**—Have each student make a flash card for each combining form on pages 361–362 of the textbook. Each flash card should show the combining form on the front and have the definition and at least two examples on the back. See page viii of this manual for instructions.

2. **Using Resources**—Have each student or student group choose one part of the female reproductive system. Instruct them to use the library and the Internet to list functions of and potential diseases that may occur in that part. Have them report to the class if possible.

3. **Creative Thinking**—Using the form below, have students make up a chart for an obstetrician's patient from initial visit to determine pregnancy through the pregnancy to delivery. Have them list procedures, approximate dates, complications, and any special notes.

Patient Name _____ Date _____

ID # _____ Date of Birth _____ Date of last menstrual period _____

Date   Time   Notes

_____

_____

_____

_____

_____

4. **Practicing Pronunciation**—Have students read the Chapter Review list out loud either together or sequentially. Stop and correct any mistakes in pronunciation. (Self-study students and distance learners can refer to the audiotapes and CD-ROM and compare their pronunciations to the ones given.)

5. **Reinforcing Spelling**—With books closed, have students spell selected words that you read aloud to them from the Chapter Review list. Have any student who spells a word incorrectly write it on the blackboard or a piece of paper 10 times. (Self-study students and distance learners should use the audiotapes or the CD-ROM, by covering the screen and listening to the audio only, to test themselves. They should write down the words as they listen and check their spelling against the text.)

6. **Learning the Roots**—Read aloud female reproductive system words that are made up of word parts. Have students name the parts and define the words. (Self-study students and distance learners should use the Chapter Review lists to pick out words that can be divided into word parts. They should write the word parts and check them in the chapter itself or in a medical dictionary.)

7. **Using Medical Documents**—Choose a medical document from the section starting on page 91 of this Instructor's Manual. Ask students questions about the document to see if they comprehend the information. (Supply distance learners with a medical document and have them fill out as much as they can, providing information for a person with a female reproductive system disease.)

8. **Learning Terms**—Have students watch a medically oriented television show and listen for at least three medical terms (preferably about the female reproductive system). Write down the terms and their meanings.

9. **Building a Case Study**—As an end-of-chapter project, have the class build a case study. They can start with a patient with female reproductive system pathology. Have them each build a part of the patient's file showing doctor's notes about the initial visits, tests requested, results, and treatments. Each student may be assigned a role in the development of the case study. (Self-study students or distance learners can use the Internet to write a short part of a case study about a patient with a particular disease.)

10. **Newsworthy Notes**—Have each student bring in one newspaper article (or even an advertisement) or an Internet printout about female reproductive system health. Students should discuss the article briefly in class.

Chapter 10: Word-Building (20 questions—5 pts. each)

Using the following combining forms, complete the word that best fits the definition of each word relating to the female reproductive system listed below. Combining forms may be used more than once.

amni(o)	gynec(o)	metr(o)	salping(o)
cervic(o)	lact(o)	oo	vagin(o)
colp(o)	lacti	oophor(o)	vulv(o)
episi(o)	mamm(o)	ov(i)	
galact(o)	men(o)	perine(o)	

1. Surgical construction of a vagina: _____ poiesis.

2. Suppression of menstruation: _____ schesis.

3. Imaging of the breast: _____ graphy.

4. Narrowing of the vulva: _____ stenosis.

5. Perineal hernia: _____ cele.

6. Egg-shaped: _____ form.

7. Tubal pregnancy: _____ cyesis.

8. Relating to the cervix and bladder: _____ vesical.

9. Fungal vaginal infection: _____ mycosis.

10. Incision into the vulva: _____ tomy.

11. Inflammation of the vulva: _____ itis.

12. Uterine discharge: _____ rrhea.

13. Study and treatment of the female reproductive system: _____ logy.

14. Vaginal pain: _____ dynia.

15. Immature ovum: _____ cyte.

16. White nipple discharge: _____ rrhea.

17. Ovarian hemorrhage: _____ rhagia.

18. Inflammation of the uterus and fallopian tubes: _____ salpingitis.

19. First signs of menses: _____ phania.

20. Aspiration of fluid from the amniotic sac: _____ centesis.

Figure 10.1. Crossword for Chapter 10. Answers are on page 89 of this Instructor's Manual.

CLUES

ACROSS

4. Release of an ovum
6. X-ray imaging of the breast
10. Backward turn of the uterus
12. Two folds of skin between the labia majora
14. Lack of menstruation
15. Birth
17. Top portion of the uterus
19. Mammary gland
21. _____ pubis
22. Innermost sac membrane
24. _____ smear
25. Outermost sac membrane
27. Placenta and membranes expelled after birth
29. Premature ending of a pregnancy
30. Female reproductive organ
31. Toxic infection during pregnancy

DOWN

1. Surgical removal of a breast
2. Of the sac
3. Agent that destroys sperm
5. External female genitalia
7. Specialist in treating the female reproductive system
8. Area surrounding the nipple
9. Benign uterine tumor
11. Apex of breast
13. Bending backward of the uterus
15. Period preceding menopause
16. Specialist in treating disorders of pregnancy and birth
18. Of the uterus
19. Agent or method that prevents fertilization
20. Production of breast milk
23. Narrow area at the bottom of the uterus
24. Stage when secondary sex characteristics develop
26. Sex cell
28. Delivery of infant

Chapter 11 The Male Reproductive System

Teaching Suggestions

In addition to the general discussion of teaching by body systems in the introduction to this instructor's manual, the following suggestions provide specific class activities. For instructors involved in distance learning, you may want to assign some of these as self-directed student activities.

1. **Building Vocabulary**—Have each student make a flash card for each combining form on page 392 of the textbook. Each flash card should show the combining form on the front and have the definition and at least two examples on the back. See page viii of this manual for instructions.

2. **Using Resources**—Have each student or student group choose one part of the male reproductive system. Instruct them to use the library and the Internet to list functions of and potential diseases that may occur in that part. Have them report to the class if possible.

3. **Creative Thinking**—Have students research male infertility. Have them use the library, the Internet, or personal interviews to find out about treatments and potential for success. Then have students make up fictional patients and discuss their particular type of infertility and whether or not they were able to be helped.

4. **Practicing Pronunciation**—Have students read the Chapter Review list out loud either together or sequentially. Stop and correct any mistakes in pronunciation. (Self-study students and distance learners can refer to the audiotapes and CD-ROM and compare their pronunciations to the ones given.)

5. **Reinforcing Spelling**—With books closed, have students spell selected words that you read aloud to them from the Chapter Review list. Have any student who spells a word incorrectly write it on the blackboard or a piece of paper 10 times. (Self-study students and distance learners should use the audiotapes or the CD-ROM, by covering the screen and listening to the audio only, to test themselves. They should write down the words as they listen and check their spelling against the text.)

6. **Learning the Roots**—Read aloud male reproductive system words that are made up of word parts. Have students name the parts and define the words. (Self-study students and distance learners should use the Chapter

Review lists to pick out words that can be divided into word parts. They should write the word parts and check them in the chapter itself or in a medical dictionary.)

7. **Using Medical Documents**—Choose a medical document from the section starting on page 91 of this Instructor's Manual. Ask students questions about the document to see if they comprehend the information. (Supply distance learners with a medical document and have them fill out as much as they can, providing information for a person with a male reproductive system disease.)

8. **Learning Terms**—Have students watch a medically oriented television show and listen for at least three medical terms (preferably about the male reproductive system). Write down the terms and their meanings.

9. **Building a Case Study**—As an end-of-chapter project, have the class build a case study. They can start with a patient with male reproductive system pathology. Have them each build a part of the patient's file showing doctor's notes about the initial visits, tests requested, results, and treatments. Each student may be assigned a role in the development of the case study. (Self-study students or distance learners can use the Internet to write a short part of a case study about a patient with a particular disease.)

10. **Newsworthy Notes**—Have each student bring in one newspaper article (or even an advertisement) or an Internet printout about male reproductive system health. Students should discuss the article briefly in class.

Name _____ Date _____

Chapter 11: Word-Building (20 questions—5 pts. each)

Using the following combining forms, complete the word that best fits the definition of each word relating to the male reproductive system listed below. Combining forms may be used more than once.

andr(o)   orch(o)   prostat(o)
balan(o)   orchi(o)   sperm(o)
epididym(o)   orchid(o)   spermat(o)

1. Male testicular tumor: _____ blastoma.

2. Involuntary movement of the testis: _____ chorea.

3. Removal of the epididymis: _____ ectomy.

4. Inflammation of the glans penis: _____ itis.

5. Enlargement of the prostate: _____ megaly.

6. Surgical moving of an undescended testis: _____ pexy.

7. Having both male and female characteristics: _____ gyny.

8. Inflammation of the prostate and bladder: _____ cystitis.

9. Incision into a testis: _____ tomy.

10. Stone in the prostate: _____ lith.

11. Surgical removal of the epididymis and the vas deferens: _____ vasectomy.

12. Sperm-bearing: _____ phore.

13. Stimulating growth of male sex organs: _____ gen.

14. Destruction of sperm: _____ lysis.

15. Testicular disease: _____ tis.

16. Incision into the epididymis: _____ tomy.

17. Primitive sperm cell: _____ gonium.

18. Repair of the glans penis: _____ plasty.

19. Agent that destroys sperm: _____ cide.

20. Abnormal prostatic discharge: _____ rrhea.

```
b  u  l  b  o  u  r  e  t  h  r  a  l  r  e  t  h  h  p  r  g
u  a  o  a  r  l  e  p  r  o  s  t  a  t  e  p  r  e  e  e  l
l  n  l  l  c  t  s  i  m  p  o  t  e  n  c  e  s  r  y  t  a
a  o  i  a  h  r  e  s  e  i  r  e  t  e  r  r  t  n  r  e  n
n  r  g  n  n  a  c  p  a  r  c  s  k  i  d  i  e  i  o  r  s
i  c  o  t  i  i  c  a  t  o  h  t  y  e  n  n  p  a  n  g  p
t  h  s  i  d  s  t  d  i  n  i  i  l  l  i  e  i  n  i  u  e
r  u  p  s  i  o  i  i  s  y  d  s  t  r  u  u  d  a  e  h  n
t  s  e  p  o  m  o  a  s  p  e  r  m  i  a  m  i  b  s  t  i
e  m  r  o  y  n  n  s  r  e  c  h  o  i  k  l  d  o  d  r  s
s  e  m  e  n  o  m  t  u  y  t  r  b  u  l  b  y  l  i  h  e
t  r  i  n  b  c  r  y  p  t  o  r  c  h  i  s  m  i  s  r  m
o  v  a  r  p  r  i  p  i  s  m  s  i  o  p  r  i  c  e  o  n
s  o  v  a  s  e  c  t  o  m  y  u  r  e  t  h  s  o  a  m  o
t  s  a  m  n  i  n  o  f  l  a  g  e  l  l  u  m  i  s  a  v
e  o  r  t  r  e  g  i  n  f  e  r  t  i  l  i  t  y  e  r  a
r  v  i  p  r  i  v  a  s  d  e  f  e  r  e  n  s  i  f  g  s
o  a  c  e  j  a  c  u  l  a  t  i  o  n  i  c  r  t  o  r  o
n  s  o  n  h  y  d  r  o  c  e  l  e  s  r  e  t  r  r  t  v
e  o  c  e  l  o  p  r  t  y  u  i  o  o  p  o  i  u  e  h  a
e  v  e  m  a  s  s  p  e  r  m  a  t  o  g  e  n  e  s  i  s
y  a  l  u  s  i  t  i  c  o  u  u  l  o  p  u  h  j  k  o  o
o  s  e  j  a  i  m  p  h  i  m  o  s  i  s  t  i  s  i  k  s
n  e  m  i  s  t  p  e  r  o  t  h  r  o  p  l  o  i  n  i  t
s  e  m  e  n  a  n  a  l  y  s  i  s  e  e  s  e  s  t  d  o
i  t  r  i  g  u  n  e  i  m  p  o  t  e  r  c  y  r  t  e  m
e  m  a  j  u  r  e  t  h  r  o  g  r  a  m  e  a  t  r  e  y
c  a  s  t  r  a  t  i  o  n  p  y  s  e  m  i  n  o  m  a  s
```

Figure 11.1. Word Find for Chapter 11.   Circle at least 20 words in this puzzle that are listed in the Chapter 11 Review section of the textbook. Answers are on page 89 of this Instructor's Manual.

Chapter 12 The Blood System

Teaching Suggestions

In addition to the general discussion of teaching by body systems in the introduction to this Instructor's Manual, the following suggestions provide specific class activities. For instructors involved in distance learning, you may want to assign some of these as self-directed student activities.

1. **Building Vocabulary**—Have each student make a flash card for each combining form on page 422 of the textbook. Each flash card should show the combining form on the front and have the definition and at least two examples on the back. See page viii of this manual for instructions.

2. **Using Resources**—Have each student or student group choose one part of the blood system. Instruct them to use the library and the Internet to list functions of and potential diseases that may occur in that part. Have them report to the class if possible.

3. **Creative Thinking**—Have students make up three patients with different forms of leukemia. Have the students discuss the symptoms, possible treatments, and likely outcomes for each of the three patients. Students should gather information from the chapter as well as from the Internet and the library.

4. **Practicing Pronunciation**—Have students read the Chapter Review list out loud either together or sequentially. Stop and correct any mistakes in pronunciation. (Self-study students and distance learners can refer to the audiotapes and CD-ROM and compare their pronunciations to the ones given.)

5. **Reinforcing Spelling**—With books closed, have students spell selected words that you read aloud to them from the Chapter Review list. Have any student who spells a word incorrectly write it on the blackboard or a piece of paper 10 times. (Self-study students and distance learners should use the audiotapes or the CD-ROM, by covering the screen and listening to the audio only, to test themselves. They should write down the words as they listen and check their spelling against the text.)

6. **Learning the Roots**—Read aloud blood system words that are made up of word parts. Have students name the parts and define the words. (Self-study students and distance learners should use the Chapter Review lists to pick out words that can be divided into word parts. They should write the word parts and check them in the chapter itself or in a medical dictionary.)

7. **Using Medical Documents**—Choose a medical document from the section starting on page 91 of this Instructor's Manual. Ask students questions about the document to see if they comprehend the information. (Supply distance learners with a medical document and have them fill out as much as they can, providing information for a person with a blood system disease.)

8. **Learning Terms**—Have students watch a medically oriented television show and listen for at least three medical terms (preferably about the blood system). Write down the terms and their meanings.

9. **Building a Case Study**—As an end-of-chapter project, have the class build a case study. They can start with a blood bank and talk about types of blood, their rarity, and the need for blood donations from healthy people. Each student may be assigned a role in the development of the case study. (Self-study students or distance learners can use the Internet to write a short part of a case study about issues relating to blood banks.)

10. **Newsworthy Notes**—Have each student bring in one newspaper article (or even an advertisement) or an Internet printout about the nation's blood supply. Students should discuss the article briefly in class.

Name _____ Date _____

Chapter 12: Word-Building (20 questions—5 pts. each)

Using the following combining forms, complete the word that best fits the definition of each word relating to the blood system listed below. Combining forms may be used more than once.

agglutin(o)	hemat(o)
eosino	leuk(o)
erythr(o)	phag(o)
hemo	thromb(o)

1. Deficiency of eosinophils: _____ penia.

2. Cleansing of the blood: _____ catharsis.

3. Excess blood in the bladder: _____ cystis.

4. Formation of red blood cells: _____ poiesis.

5. White blood cell: _____ cyte.

6. Stimulating the formation of agglutinin: _____ genic.

7. Hemorrhage into spinal fluid: _____ myelia.

8. Vision abnormality with objects appearing red: _____ opsia.

9. Removal of white blood cells: _____ apheresis.

10. Reddening of the skin: _____ derma.

11. Cell that ingests things: _____ cyte.

12. Dialysis with removal of substances from the blood: _____ dialysis.

13. Producing red: _____ genic.

14. Medical specialty concerned with the blood system: _____ logy.

15. Destruction of red blood cells: _____ phagia.

16. Inflammation of veins with thrombi: _____ phlebitis.

17. Excessive fear of eating: _____ phobia.

18. Fragmentation of red blood cells: _____ clasis.

19. Death of vessel walls due to a thrombus: _____ necrosis.

20. Disorder with excessive white blood cells: _____ emia.

```
b l o o d c u l t u r e m i s s i o n o k
i e o b l o o d i n d i c e s i d u h g i
o r d o o m p t h r o m b o u i y e n n l
c y c n u p l a s m a b l s m b s m p l o
h t h e p l a t e l e t o i p k c y r i p
e h e m c e t s h y s r t n r i r t o m o
m r n a h t e i r m y e l o b l a s t i i
i o m r e e l k m p r y u p u r s i h t k
s p i r m b e c b h t r h h r t i s r r l
t o s o s l t l i o p o i i p s a t o h c
r e p w e o c e n c k i l l u i h e m e y
y t o b l o o d t y p e h e p s e m b l t
p i i l o d u u i t h e m n u o m i i e o
a n k y l c n m n e c y r d r t o a n c s
n p i r t o t r e m o r e n p i g n e t u
e o l l e u k e m i a l l e u c l m m r y
l i o d r n e m i a g u a n r s o t i o i
y e c y h t h r o m u s p m a i b h a p o
m t y s f r a n h u l k s k l n i r t h g
p h t c a d e r u m a n e m i a n d p o h
j r o r c e b g r a n u l o c y t e o r j
k o s s t e m c e l l a l l e r u i o e k
a n i s o c y t o s i s h e m o g e n s l
n o s t r b o o d l o h e m o s t a t i c
g p o l y c y t h e m i a n i s o c y s m
g r a n u l o c y t o s i s g r t y u i b
i r r e t i c u l o c y t o s i s i s t i
n f t h a l a s s e m i a t h r o m b u n
```

Figure 12.1. Word Find for Chapter 12. Circle at least 20 words in this puzzle that are listed in the Chapter 12 Review section of the textbook. Answers are on page 89 of this Instructor's Manual.

Chapter 13   The Lymphatic and Immune Systems

In addition to the general discussion of teaching by body systems in the introduction to this Instructor's Manual, the following suggestions provide specific class activities. For instructors involved in distance learning, you may want to assign some of these as self-directed student activities.

1. **Building Vocabulary**—Have each student make a flash card for each combining form on page 454 of the textbook. Each flash card should show the combining form on the front and have the definition and at least two examples on the back. See page viii of this manual for instructions.

2. **Using Resources**—Have each student or student group choose one part of the lymphatic and immune systems. Instruct them to use the library and the Internet to list functions of and potential diseases that may occur in that part. Have them report to the class if possible.

3. **Creative Thinking**—Have students research HIV and AIDS. Have some students discuss the history of the disease and how the worldwide epidemic is currently being handled. Have them discuss ways in which HIV is spread, treatments, ethical issues, and complications of AIDS.

4. **Practicing Pronunciation**—Have students read the Chapter Review list out loud either together or sequentially. Stop and correct any mistakes in pronunciation. (Self-study students and distance learners can refer to the audiotapes and CD-ROM and compare their pronunciations to the ones given.)

5. **Reinforcing Spelling**—With books closed, have students spell selected words that you read aloud to them from the Chapter Review list. Have any student who spells a word incorrectly write it on the blackboard or a piece of paper 10 times. (Self-study students and distance learners should use the audiotapes or the CD-ROM, by covering the screen and listening to the audio only, to test themselves. They should write down the words as they listen and check their spelling against the text.)

6. **Learning the Roots**—Read aloud lymphatic and immune systems words that are made up of word parts. Have students name the parts and define the words. (Self-study students and distance learners should use the Chapter Review lists to pick out words that can be divided into word parts. They should write the word parts and check them in the chapter itself or in a medical dictionary.)

7. **Using Medical Documents**—Choose a medical document from the section starting on page 91 of this Instructor's Manual. Ask students questions about the document to see if they comprehend the information. (Supply distance learners with a medical document and have them fill out as much as they can, providing information for a person with a lymphatic or immune system disease.)

8. **Learning Terms**—Have students watch a medically oriented television show and listen for at least three medical terms (preferably about the lymphatic or immune system). Write down the terms and their meanings.

9. **Building a Case Study**—As an end-of-chapter project, have the class build a case study. They can start with a patient with AIDS. Have them each build a part of the patient's file showing doctor's notes about the initial visits, tests requested, results, and treatments. Each student may be assigned a role in the development of the case study. (Self-study students or distance learners can use the Internet to write a short part of a case study about a patient with a particular AIDS complication.)

10. **Newsworthy Notes**—Have each student bring in one newspaper article (or even an advertisement) or an Internet printout about HIV or AIDS research. Students should discuss the article briefly in class.

Chapter 13:   Word-Building (20 questions—5 pts. each)

Using the following combining forms, complete the word that best fits the definition of each word relating to the lymphatic and immune systems listed below. Combining forms may be used more than once.

aden(o)   splen(o)
immun(o)   thym(o)
lymph(o)   tox(o)
lymphaden(o)   toxi
lymphangi(o)   toxico

1. Cell formed in lymph: _____ cyte.

2. Agent that suppresses an immune response: _____ suppressant.

3. Imaging of lymph nodes: _____ ography.

4. Discharge of lymph into urine: _____ uria.

5. Glandular tumor: _____ oma.

6. Hernia in the spleen: _____ cele.

7. Circulation of lymph: _____ kinesis.

8. Cell that develops in the thymus: _____ cyte.

9. Inflammation of lymph nodes: _____ itis.

10. Therapy that stimulates the immune system: _____ therapy.

11. Tumor in thymal tissue: _____ oma.

12. Obstruction of lymph flow: _____ stasis.

13. Morbid fear of poisoning: _____ phobia.

14. Glandular cell: _____ cyte.

15. Susceptible to poisons: _____ phil.

16. Formation of lymphatic tissue: _____ poiesis.

17. Poisonous: _____ ferous.

18. Muscle tumor with glandular parts: _____ myoma.

19. Anemia resulting from a poison: _____ anemia.

20. Enlarged spleen: _____ megaly.

```
r s a n a p h y l a x i s p l e n n o m e
m e t a s t a s i s p l n e e p f g h k l
n t t h y m o m a a n t i g e n r o t e r
a s p r e t h m a r p h s p l e i m k l j
t p a m o m l o p c r e t y u i m o p l l
u l n o n v e n n o r e t r o k m o p t y
r e t n j a i d s i t o y u i o u t r o m
a n i o k c m r u d i s p l e e n n n l p
l o b n l c m p u i m k l h o l i y m p h
i r o u o i s u s m k l l a o t m l a o
m e d c l n n e r i n g o u i g y m p l c
m t y l m a u f u s p l e n o m e g a l y
u r u e o t m p e h e d e n o l p l m e t
n o i o p i i n i c m m u n i m p l m r e
i l n s y o p p o r t u n i s t i c i g y
t o t i r n m a l i k i l l o p n a t e r
y y e s r e l t g a n m o p l y f u m n u
t m r y t e r h i v s t i u g h e t u i i
r p f m r n e o m l y m p h s i c o l l t
e o e m e o m g m r u p a i i p t i i h y
d m r u t m m e u e m h l k s o i m m p m
o h o d g k i n s t m y l l o i o m p m m
n g n h y o n r t y i m e o m y n u h y u
h a i h u m o r a l t p r p i u k n o t n
p k t h y m u s o m a m g o y j l e c i i
m o y l i m p h a g o c y t o s i s t r g
y h y p e r s e n s i t i v i t y r t y h
l y m p h a d e n o p a t h y h j k l s e
```

Figure 13.1. Word Find for Chapter 13. Circle at least 20 words in this puzzle that are listed in the Chapter 13 Review section of the textbook. Answers are on page 90 of this Instructor's Manual.

Chapter 14 The Digestive System

In addition to the general discussion of teaching by body systems in the introduction to this Instructor's Manual, the following suggestions provide specific class activities. For instructors involved in distance learning, you may want to assign some of these as self-directed student activities.

1. **Building Vocabulary**—Have each student make a flash card for each combining form on pages 484–486 of the textbook. Each flash card should show the combining form on the front and have the definition and at least two examples on the back. See page viii of this manual for instructions.

2. **Using Resources**—Have each student or student group choose one part of the digestive system. Instruct them to use the library and the Internet to list functions of and potential diseases that may occur in that part. Have them report to the class if possible.

3. **Creative Thinking**—Using the form below, have students choose a digestive disease and make up a fictional series medical chart for a person with that disease. Have them list symptoms, potential treatments, and outlook.

Patient Name _____   Date _____

ID # _____   Date of Birth _____   Insurance carrier _____

Date   Time of Visit   Notes

_____

_____

_____

_____

_____

_____

4. **Practicing Pronunciation**—Have students read the Chapter Review list out loud either together or sequentially. Stop and correct any mistakes in pronunciation. (Self-study students and distance learners can refer to the audiotapes and CD-ROM and compare their pronunciations to the ones given.)

5. **Reinforcing Spelling**—With books closed, have students spell selected words that you read aloud to them from the Chapter Review list. Have any student who spells a word incorrectly write it on the blackboard or a piece of paper 10 times. (Self-study students and distance learners should use the audiotapes or the CD-ROM, by covering the screen and listening to the audio only, to test themselves. They should write down the words as they listen and check their spelling against the text.)

6. **Learning the Roots**—Read aloud digestive system words that are made up of word parts. Have students name the parts and define the words. (Self-study students and distance learners should use the Chapter Review lists to pick out words that can be divided into word parts. They should write the word parts and check them in the chapter itself or in a medical dictionary.)

7. **Using Medical Documents**—Choose a medical document from the section starting on page 91 of this Instructor's Manual. Ask students questions about the document to see if they comprehend the information. (Supply distance learners with a medical document and have them fill out as much as they can providing information for a person with an digestive system disease.)

8. **Learning Terms**—Have students watch a medically oriented television show and listen for at least three medical terms (preferably about the digestive system). Write down the terms and their meanings.

9. **Building a Case Study**—As an end-of-chapter project, have the class build a case study. They can start with their own diets and discuss what digestive system diseases might require them to modify their own diets. They should research other digestive system diseases and how dietary and nutritional items play a role in the symptoms of the disease. (Self-study students or distance learners can use the Internet to write a short part of a case study about the diet of a patient with a particular disease.)

10. **Newsworthy Notes**—Have each student bring in one newspaper article (or even an advertisement) or an Internet printout about digestive system health. Students should discuss the article briefly in class.

Figure 14.1. Crossword for Chapter 14. Answers are on page 90 of this Instructor's Manual.

CLUES

ACROSS

1. Condition with tongue attached incorrectly
6. Raised area on tongue
10. Projection from soft palate
11. Of the liver
12. Place at which feces exits body
14. Bottom part of small intestine
17. _____ intestine
18. Pouch at the top of the large intestine
20. Pharynx
22. _____ intestine
23. Fleshy part of mouth that moves
26. Semisolid mass in stomach
27. Agent that relieves constipation
29. Inflammation of the bile ducts
31. Eating disorder
32. Laxative
33. Connects pharynx to stomach

DOWN

2. Sick feeling
3. Organ that secretes bile
4. Fat in the blood
5. Inflammation of the ileum
7. Agent that prevents emesis
8. Pancreatic enzyme
9. _____ canal
13. Place where food is broken down
15. Inflammation of the intestines
16. Belching
18. Removal of gallbladder
19. Membrane that attaches intestines to the abdominal wall
21. Appendage
24. Twisted intestinal blockage
25. Appendix
26. Combining form for the common bile duct
28. Secreted by liver
30. _____ palate

Chapter 14: Word-Building (20 questions—5 pts. each)

Using the following combining forms, complete the word that best fits the definition of each word relating to the digestive system listed below. Combining forms may be used more than once.

an(o)	chol(e)	gluc(o)	rect(o)
append(o)	colon(o)	glyc(o)	sial(o)
bil(i)	duoden(o)	hepat(o)	sigmoid(o)
bucc(o)	enter(o)	labi(o)	steat(o)
cec(o)	gastr(o)	lingu(o)	stomat(o)

1. Bile-producing: _____ genic.

2. Away from the liver: _____ fugal.

3. Tending to mobilize sugars: _____ kinetic.

4. Affecting the intestine: _____ tropic.

5. Surgical anchoring of the cecum: _____ pexy.

6. Chronic lip spasms: _____ chorea.

7. Gallstone: _____ lith.

8. Hernia in the rectum: _____ cele.

9. Narrowing of the intestine: _____ stenosis.

10. Lining of the anal canal: _____ derm.

11. Inflammation of the stomach and colon: _____ colitis.

12. Disease of the mouth: _____ pathy.

13. Tumor of the bile duct: _____ angioma.

14. Surgical opening of the sigmoid colon: _____ ostomy.

15. Removal of the appendix: _____ ectomy.

16. Poisonous to the liver: _____ toxic.

17. Secretion of fat in the stool: _____ rrhea.

18. Dilation of the stomach: _____ ectasis.

19. Visual examination of the colon: _____ scopy.

20. Mouth pain: _____ algia.

Chapter 15 The Endocrine System

Teaching Suggestions

In addition to the general discussion of teaching by body systems in the introduction to this Instructor's Manual, the following suggestions provide specific class activities. For instructors involved in distance learning, you may want to assign some of these as self-directed student activities.

1. **Building Vocabulary**—Have each student make a flash card for each combining form on page 525 of the textbook. Each flash card should show the combining form on the front and have the definition and at least two examples on the back. See page viii of this manual for instructions.

2. **Using Resources**—Have each student or student group choose one part of the endocrine system. Instruct them to use the library and the Internet to list functions of and potential diseases that may occur in that part. Have them report to the class if possible.

3. **Creative Thinking**—Using the form below, have students chart a patient with Type I diabetes and make up a fictional series medical chart for a person with that disease. Have them list symptoms, potential treatments, and outlook.

Patient Name _____ Date _____

ID# _____ Date of Birth _____ Insurance carrier _____

Date   Time of Visit   Notes

_____

_____

_____

_____

_____

_____

4. **Practicing Pronunciation**—Have students read the Chapter Review list out loud either together or sequentially. Stop and correct any mistakes in pronunciation. (Self-study students and distance learners can refer to the audiotapes and CD-ROM and compare their pronunciations to the ones given.)

5. **Reinforcing Spelling**—With books closed, have students spell selected words that you read aloud to them from the Chapter Review list. Have any student who spells a word incorrectly write it on the blackboard or a piece of paper 10 times. (Self-study students and distance learners should use the audiotapes or the CD-ROM, by covering the screen and listening to the audio only to test themselves. They should write down the words as they listen and check their spelling against the text.)

6. **Learning the Roots**—Read aloud endocrine system words that are made up of word parts. Have students name the parts and define the words. (Self-study students and distance learners should use the Chapter Review lists to pick out words that can be divided into word parts. They should write the word parts and check them in the chapter itself or in a medical dictionary.)

7. **Using Medical Documents**—Choose a medical document from the section starting on page 91 of this Instructor's Manual. Ask students questions about the document to see if they comprehend the information. (Supply distance learners with a medical document and have them fill out as much as they can, providing information for a person with an endocrine system disease.)

8. **Learning Terms**—Have students watch a medically oriented television show and listen for at least three medical terms (preferably about the endocrine system). Write down the terms and their meanings.

9. **Building a Case Study**—As an end-of-chapter project, have the class build a case study. They should compare the histories, symptoms, treatments of outlooks of two patients—one with Type I diabetes and one with Type II. They should research some of the gene therapies now being discussed and how they will impact the course of each disease. (Self-study students or distance learners can use the Internet to write a short part of a case study about a patient with Type I or Type II diabetes.)

10. **Newsworthy Notes**—Have each student bring in one newspaper article (or even advertisement) or an Internet printout about endocrine system health. Students should discuss the article briefly in class.

Chapter 15: Word-Building (20 questions—5 pts. each)

Using the following combining forms, complete the word that best fits the definition of each word relating to endocrine system listed below. Combining forms may be used more than once.

aden(o)	gonad(o)
adren(o)	pancreat(o)
adrenal(o)	parathyroid(o)
gluc(o)	thyr(o)
glyc(o)	thyroid(o)

1. Formation of sugar: _____ genesis.

2. Calculus in the pancreas: _____ lith.

3. Surgical removal of a gland: _____ ectomy.

4. Causing destruction of thyroid cells: _____ lytic.

5. Relating to the gonads: _____ al.

6. Excision of an ovary or testis: _____ ectomy.

7. Enlargement of the adrenal glands: _____ megaly.

8. Inflammation of the thyroid: _____ itis.

9. Acting on the pancreas: _____ tropic.

10. Thyroid repair: _____ plasty.

11. Glandular tumor: _____ oma.

12. Glandular tumor in the muscles: _____ myoma.

13. Arising from the pancreas: _____ genic.

14. Incision into the thyroid: _____ tomy.

15. Inflammation of the adrenal glands: _____ itis.

16. Imaging of the pancreatic ducts: _____ graphy.

17. Thyroid disorder: _____ pathy.

18. Gland-forming cell: _____ blast.

19. Stimulating the thyroid: _____ tropic.

20. Benign glandular tumor: _____ lymphoma.

```
a c r o m e g a l y t r e c e p t o r a m
l n s g o i t e r i s m y x e d h m n n e
d e t h y r o t o x i n e x e c y r y t l
o u d i a b e t e s t e a t r r r i o i a
s r s p h h y p e r d i a u t i o i i h n
t o u o h y p e r t h y r o i d i s m y o
e h p i y p p i t u i t a r y u d t e p c
r i r g l o e o g l y c m i a u j h l o y
o p a l l s r k g l u c a g o n i m a g t
n g r o i e s d f l u t i o m u t u t l e
e o e g i c e s t h y m u s i v f s o y s
u i n i n r c h o l r c y s o l o m n c t
r t a r g e t c e l l k e t o s i s i e i
o e l t e t h y u i k l i m o m a r n m m
h r r a d i o a c t i v e l i g n d c i u
y o e n s o m a t r o p h i c c d i e c l
p i l d t n e n d o h i u r s t r o d a a
o d e r u r t e s t i c l e i k j a h l t
p r a y m e a n d r r o g e a o u d t p i
h h s g p g l u c o s e n m n l o r i a n
y t i h j y u o i t u j k l d i l e l c g
s r n y k e g r o w t h h o r m o n e e h
i y g n l n e r t y i k l p o o m a d l o
s r a r n d r o u m s t e r g i p l o l r
i e g i g a n t i s m r e l e i u i l l m
s t i e r m y x e d e m a h n m o n e s o
d i a b e t i c m e l l i t u s i e r t n
p o s t p r a n d i a l i e n i r c o x e
```

Figure 15.1. Word Find for Chapter 15. Circle at least 20 words in this puzzle that are listed in the Chapter 15 Review section of the textbook. Answers are on page 90 of this Instructor's Manual.

Chapter 16 The Sensory System

In addition to the general discussion of teaching by body systems in the introduction to this Instructor's Manual, the following suggestions provide specific class activities. For instructors involved in distance learning, you may want to assign some of these as self-directed student activities.

1. **Building Vocabulary**—Have each student make a flash card for each combining form on pages 559–560 of the textbook. Each flash card should show the combining form on the front and have the definition and at least two examples on the back. See page viii of this manual for instructions.

2. **Using Resources**—Have each student or student group choose one part of the sensory system. Instruct them to use the library and the Internet to list functions of and potential diseases that may occur in that part. Have them report to the class if possible.

3. **Creative Thinking**—Divide the students into five groups. Have each group concentrate on one of the five senses. Discuss the functions of each sense, potential diseases, and what the loss of that sense would mean. Have students work out ways to compensate for the loss of one or more of the senses.

4. **Practicing Pronunciation**—Have students read the Chapter Review list out loud either together or sequentially. Stop and correct any mistakes in pronunciation. (Self-study students and distance learners can refer to the audiotapes and CD-ROM and compare their pronunciations to the ones given.)

5. **Reinforcing Spelling**—With books closed, have students spell selected words that you read aloud to them from the Chapter Review list. Have any student who spells a word incorrectly write it on the blackboard or a piece of paper 10 times. (Self-study students and distance learners should use the audiotapes or the CD-ROM, by covering the screen and listening to the audio only, to test themselves. They should write down the words as they listen and check their spelling against the text.)

6. **Learning the Roots**—Read aloud sensory system words that are made up of word parts. Have students name the parts and define the words. (Self-study students and distance learners should use the Chapter Review lists to pick out words that can be divided into word parts. They should write the word parts and check them in the chapter itself or in a medical dictionary.)

7. **Using Medical Documents**—Choose a medical document from the section starting on page 91 of this Instructor's Manual. Ask students questions about the document to see if they comprehend the information. (Supply distance learners with a medical document and have them fill out as much as they can, providing information for a person with a sensory system disease or deficiency.)

8. **Learning Terms**—Have students watch a medically oriented television show and listen for at least three medical terms (preferably about the sensory system). Write down the terms and their meanings.

9. **Building a Case Study**—As an end-of-chapter project, have the class build a case study. They should compare five patients, each with a disease of a different sense. Track the severity of the impact of each disease on the life of the patient being studied. Discuss some resources available to people with sensory system diseases or deficiencies. (Self-study students or distance learners can use the Internet to write a short part of a case study about a patient with a sensory system disease or deficiency.)

10. **Newsworthy Notes**—Have each student bring in one newspaper article (or even an advertisement) or an Internet printout about sensory system health. Students should discuss the article briefly in class.

Chapter 16: Word-Building (20 questions—5 pts. each)

Using the following combining forms, complete the word that best fits the definition of each word relating to the sensory system listed below. Combining forms may be used more than once.

audi(o)	cor(o)	myring(o)	pupill(o)
blephar(o)	corne(o)	nas(o)	retin(o)
cerumin(o)	dacry(o)	ophthalm(o)	scler(o)
cochle(o)	ir(o)	ossicul(o)	scot(o)
conjunctiv(o)	lacrim(o)	phac(o)	uve(o)

1. Abnormal positioning of the pupil: _____ ectopia.

2. Incision into the eardrum: _____ tomy.

3. Hernia of the lens: _____ cele.

4. Caused by sound: _____ genic.

5. Relating to the cochlea: _____ ar.

6. Involving the nose and stomach: _____ gastric.

7. Excessive tearing: _____ rrhea.

8. Inflammation of the conjunctiva: _____ itis.

9. Repositioning of a detached retina: _____ piesis.

10. Swelling of the eyelids: _____ edema.

11. Surgical repair of the sclera: _____ plasty.

12. Softening of the lens: _____ malacia.

13. Inflammation of the nose and sinuses: _____ sinusitis.

14. Substance that softens wax: _____ lytic.

15. Inflammation of the uvea: _____ itis.

16. Inflammation of the iris: _____ itis.

17. Fungal disease of the eye: _____ mycosis.

18. Narrowing of the tear duct: _____ stenosis.

19. Of low illumination: _____ opic.

20. Removal of the ossicle: _____ ectomy.

```
n  y  s  t  a  g  m  u  s  i  s  c  o  t  o  m  a  m  o  p  p
e  e  s  t  r  a  b  i  i  r  i  d  e  c  t  o  m  y  t  h  s
a  n  u  v  e  a  s  n  g  r  o  p  i  k  l  t  o  p  o  o  e
r  d  o  r  d  a  s  t  h  e  n  o  p  i  a  o  r  t  y  y  u
s  o  n  o  o  p  h  t  t  h  a  e  s  o  t  r  o  p  i  a  d
i  l  o  i  p  r  e  s  b  y  o  p  i  a  a  r  y  t  o  p  o
g  y  p  h  t  h  e  m  n  l  a  c  r  i  m  h  a  t  r  h  p
h  m  t  h  a  l  m  t  o  p  i  s  t  r  a  e  i  s  m  o  h
t  p  h  o  p  i  a  c  i  y  v  n  c  a  t  a  r  a  c  t  a
e  h  a  v  r  d  e  r  b  n  o  p  d  i  a  s  e  d  o  o  k
d  e  c  i  b  e  l  o  p  i  a  s  t  n  r  a  b  o  c  p  i
n  y  c  t  l  a  c  r  i  m  a  t  e  r  e  n  m  p  h  h  a
e  s  o  p  e  f  r  o  c  u  l  a  m  a  c  s  u  h  l  o  p
s  t  r  a  p  n  b  d  r  a  c  e  d  r  e  m  s  t  e  b  o
s  t  r  a  h  e  n  s  t  y  g  m  u  s  b  r  i  h  a  i  i
o  p  h  t  a  s  t  r  a  b  i  s  o  m  m  a  c  u  l  a  r
b  i  f  a  r  s  i  g  h  t  e  d  n  e  s  s  i  s  c  l  e
i  a  a  m  i  s  o  p  h  t  h  a  l  n  y  t  v  t  c  t  t
s  o  r  n  t  o  p  i  a  m  p  u  p  i  l  a  s  a  l  y  i
t  i  n  n  i  t  u  s  o  s  a  n  i  e  r  p  u  p  i  l  n
a  r  i  s  s  i  s  t  i  m  p  o  n  r  t  e  m  e  l  p  i
s  t  r  a  b  i  s  o  p  h  i  t  k  e  n  s  s  s  u  i  t
t  o  n  o  m  e  t  r  y  a  l  m  e  s  y  u  i  o  p  o  i
e  u  s  t  a  c  h  i  a  n  l  r  y  a  p  a  b  i  s  m  s
b  c  c  o  r  n  e  a  l  o  a  y  e  n  d  o  l  y  m  p  p
u  h  e  a  r  y  u  i  o  k  e  r  a  t  o  p  l  a  s  t  y
d  a  c  r  y  o  c  y  s  t  e  c  t  o  m  y  i  u  o  p  l
s  t  r  a  b  i  s  m  u  s  v  e  s  t  i  b  u  l  e  a  i
```

Figure 16.1. Word Find for Chapter 16. Circle at least 20 words in this puzzle that are listed in the Chapter 16 Review section of the textbook. Answers are on page 90 of this Instructor's Manual.

Chapter 17 Human Development

The chapter on human development attempts to tie together all the body systems in the context of the stages of development. The following suggestions provide specific class activities. For instructors involved in distance learning, you may want to assign some of these as self-directed student activities.

1. **Building Vocabulary**—Have each student make a flash card for each stage of the lifespan on pages 587–588 of the textbook. Each flash card should show the lifespan stage on the front and have the approximate ages and at least two developmental characteristics on the back.

2. **Using Resources**—Have each student or student group choose one part of the human development cycle. Instruct them to use the library and the Internet to list pathologies that may occur during that part of the cycle. Have them report to the class if possible.

3. **Creative Thinking**—Have students chart their own life cycle development giving specifics about diseases they may have had and have them imagine the next few stages of their development. Based on their family history, have them list some potential diseases that may affect them later on in life.

4. **Practicing Pronunciation**—Have students read the Chapter Review list out loud either together or sequentially. Stop and correct any mistakes in pronunciation. (Self-study students and distance learners can refer to the audiotapes and CD-ROM and compare their pronunciations to the ones given.)

5. **Reinforcing Spelling**—With books closed, have students spell selected words that you read aloud to them from the Chapter Review list. Have any student who spells a word incorrectly write it on the blackboard or a piece of paper 10 times. (Self-study students and distance learners should use the audiotapes or the CD-ROM, by covering the screen and listening to the audio only, to test themselves. They should write down the words as they listen and check their spelling against the text.)

6. **Learning the Roots**—Read aloud pathological terms of diseases common in human development that consist of word parts. Have students name the parts and define the words. (Self-study students and distance learners should use the Chapter Review lists from the various system chapters to pick out words that can be divided into word parts. They should write the word parts and check them in the chapter itself or in a medical dictionary.)

7. **Using Medical Documents**—Choose a medical document from the section starting on page 91 of this Instructor's Manual. Ask students questions about the document to see if they comprehend the information. (Supply distance learners with a medical document and have them fill out as much as they can, providing information for a person at a particular stage of human development.)

8. **Learning Terms**—Have students watch a medically oriented television show and listen for at least three medical terms (preferably about human development). Write down the terms and their meanings.

9. **Building a Case Study**—As an end-of-chapter project, have the class build a case study. They can start with a fetus and project the lifespan stages, giving the person various specific characteristics at each stage and listing pathological conditions that will occur in the fictional patient. Each student may be assigned a role in the development of the case study. (Self-study students or distance learners can use the Internet to write a short part of a case study about a patient at a particular lifespan stage.)

10. **Newsworthy Notes**—Have each student bring in one newspaper article (or even an advertisement) or an Internet printout about lifespan issues. Students should discuss the article briefly in class.

Chapter 17: Test of the Stages of Human Development (20 questions—5 pts. each)

Fill in the blanks using terms learned in Chapter 17 of the textbook. Terms may be used more than once.

1. A child from age 1 to 3 is considered a _____ .

2. Sexual intercourse may result in _____ .

3. Ages 40–59 is the period of _____ adulthood.

4. An ovum is also known as a(n) _____ .

5. The period between about age 8 to 12 is when _____ occurs.

6. The study of old age is _____ .

7. The oldest old are older than age _____ .

8. The embryo develops into a _____ after eight weeks of gestation.

9. Birth position with the head down in the birth canal is _____ .

10. Birth position with the feet first is _____ .

11. Ages 60–89 is the period of _____ .

12. Specialists in fertility, pregnancy, and birth are _____ .

13. During puberty, _____ sex characteristics develop.

14. An infant 4 weeks old or younger is called a _____ .

15. The process of readying the fetus for expulsion is called _____ .

16. Most labors end in a(n) _____ birth.

17. The period from puberty to full physical maturity is _____ .

18. Removal of the fetus through the abdomen is a(n) _____ .

19. The period of fetal development is _____ .

20. Specialists in the treatment of neonates are _____ .

Chapter 18 Terms in Oncology: Cancer and its Causes

Teaching Suggestions

The chapter on terms in oncology attempts to examine cancer as it occurs in all body systems and in all stages of development. The following suggestions provide specific class activities. For instructors involved in distance learning, you may want to assign some of these as self-directed student activities.

1. **Building Vocabulary**—Have each student make a flash card for each combining form on page 603 of the textbook. Each flash card should show the combining form on the front and have the definition and at least two examples on the back. See page viii of this manual for instructions.

2. **Using Resources**—Have each student or student group choose one type of cancer and discuss its impact on a particular body system. Instruct them to use the library and the Internet to list the characteristics of the disease they have chosen to discuss. Have them report to the class if possible.

3. **Creative Thinking**—Using the form below, have students make up a fictional medical chart for a person with the disease they chose to discuss in exercise 2. Have them list symptoms, potential treatments, and outlook.

Patient Name _____ Date _____

ID # _____ Date of Birth _____ Insurance carrier _____

Date   Time of Visit   Notes

_____

_____

_____

_____

4. **Practicing Pronunciation**—Have students read the Chapter Review list out loud either together or sequentially. Stop and correct any mistakes in pronunciation. (Self-study students and distance learners can refer to the audiotapes and CD-ROM and compare their pronunciations to the ones given.)

5. **Reinforcing Spelling**—With books closed, have students spell selected words that you read aloud to them from the Chapter Review list. Have any student who spells a word incorrectly write it on the blackboard or a piece of paper 10 times. (Self-study students and distance learners should use the audiotapes or the CD-ROM, by covering the screen and listening to the audio only, to test themselves. They should write down the words as they listen and check their spelling against the text.)

6. **Learning the Roots**—Read aloud oncological words that are made up of word parts. Have students name the parts and define the words. (Self-study students and distance learners should use the Chapter Review lists to pick out words that can be divided into word parts. They should write the word parts and check them in the chapter itself or in a medical dictionary.)

7. **Using Medical Documents**—Choose a medical document from the section starting on page 91 of this Instructor's Manual. Ask students questions about the document to see if they comprehend the information. (Supply distance learners with a medical document and have them fill out as much as they can, providing information for a person with cancer.)

8. **Learning Terms**—Have students watch a medically oriented television show and listen for at least three medical terms (preferably about oncology). Write down the terms and their meanings.

9. **Building a Case Study**—As an end-of-chapter project, have the class build a case study. They can start with an oncologist and one or two patients with cancer. Have them build part of each patient's file showing doctor's notes, tests requested, results, and treatments. Each student may be assigned a role in the development of the case study. (Self-study students or distance learners can use the Internet to write a short part of a case study about a patient with a particular cancer.)

10. **Newsworthy Notes**—Have each student bring in one newspaper article (or even advertisement) or an Internet printout about cancer prevention. Students should discuss the article briefly in class.

Name _____ Date _____

Chapter 18: Word-Building (20 questions—5 pts. each)

Using the following combining forms and suffixes, complete the word that best fits the definition of each word relating to terms in oncology listed below. Combining forms may be used more than once.

-blast	mutagen(o)	-plasm
blast(o)	-oma	-plastic
carcin(o)	onc(o)	radi(o)
muta	-plasia	

1. Cancer-causing: _____ genic.

2. Agent that promotes change: _____ gen.

3. Tumor of immature cells: _____ oma.

4. Abnormal tissue development: dys _____ .

5. Study of and treatment with radiation: _____ logy.

6. Slowing the progression of a cancer: _____ static.

7. Destructive of cancer cells: _____ lytic.

8. Radiation sickness: _____ toxemia.

9. Immature nerve cell: neuro _____ .

10. Tumor cell: _____ cyte.

11. Radiation treatment: _____ therapy.

12. Cell substance: cyto _____ .

13. Abnormal new tissue growth: neo _____ .

14. Undifferentiated cell: _____ cyte.

15. Device for measuring power of x-rays: _____ meter.

16. Destructive of a cancer tumor: _____ lytic.

17. Marked by abnormal tumor development: dys _____ .

18. Production of embryonic cells: _____ genesis.

19. Diagnosis using x-rays: _____ diagnosis.

20. Treatment of tumors: _____ therapy.

Chapter 19 Diagnostic Imaging and Surgery

The chapter on diagnostic imaging and surgery examines techniques in imaging and surgery that are widely used in diagnosis and treatment. The following suggestions provide specific class activities. For instructors involved in distance learning, you may want to assign some of these as self-directed student activities.

1. **Building Vocabulary**—Have each student make a flash card for each combining form and suffix on page 633 of the textbook. Each flash card should show the combining form on the front and have the definition and at least two examples on the back. See page viii of this manual for instructions.

2. **Using Resources**—Have each student or student group choose one type of diagnostic imaging and discuss its use for a particular body system. Instruct them to use the library and the Internet to list the advantages of the type of imaging they have chosen to discuss. Have them report to the class if possible.

3. **Creative Thinking**—Have students create a fictional patient with a disease that has been diagnosed using imaging. Have them list symptoms, potential treatments, and outlook.

4. **Practicing Pronunciation**—Have students read the Chapter Review list out loud either together or sequentially. Stop and correct any mistakes in pronunciation. (Self-study students and distance learners can refer to the audiotapes and CD-ROM and compare their pronunciations to the ones given.)

5. **Reinforcing Spelling**—With books closed, have students spell selected words that you read aloud to them from the Chapter Review list. Have any student who spells a word incorrectly write it on the blackboard or a piece of paper 10 times. (Self-study students and distance learners should use the audiotapes or the CD-ROM, by covering the screen and listening to the audio only, to test themselves. They should write down the words as they listen and check their spelling against the text.)

6. **Learning the Roots**—Read aloud diagnostic imaging and surgical terms that are made up of word parts. Have students name the parts and define the words. (Self-study students and distance learners should use the Chapter Review lists to pick out words that can be divided into word parts. They should write the word parts and check them in the chapter itself or in a medical dictionary.)

7. **Using Medical Documents**—Choose a medical document from the section starting on page 91 of this Instructor's Manual. Ask students questions about the document to see if they comprehend the information. (Supply distance learners with a medical document and have them fill out as much as they can, providing information for a person with a particular cancer treated with both radiation and surgery.)

8. **Learning Terms**—Have students watch a medically oriented television show and listen for at least three medical terms (preferably about diagnostic imaging or surgery). Write down the terms and their meanings.

9. **Building a Case Study**—As an end-of-chapter project, have the class build a case study. They can start with a radiologist and one or two patients with cancer. Have them build part of each patient's file showing doctor's notes, tests requested, results, and treatments. The patients should have imaging tests and surgery and radiation. Each student may be assigned a role in the development of the case study. (Self-study students or distance learners can use the Internet to write a short part of a case study about a patient with a particular cancer treated with both radiation and surgery.)

10. **Newsworthy Notes**—Have each student bring in one newspaper article (or even advertisement) or an Internet printout about diagnostic imaging. Students should discuss the article briefly in class.

Chapter 19: Word-Building (20 questions — 5 pts. each)

Using the following combining forms and suffixes, complete the word that best fits the definition of each word relating to diagnostic imaging and surgery listed below. Combining forms and suffixes may be used more than once.

-centesis	-gram	-pexy	-scopy
-clasis	-graphy	-plasty	son(o)
-ectomy	micr(o)	radi(o)	-stomy
electr(o)	-opsy	-rrhaphy	-tome
fluor(o)	-ostomy	-scope	-tomy

1. Surgical excision of a muscle: my _____ .

2. Making of an opening in the colon: _____ ostomy.

3. Radiograph of the heart: cardio _____ .

4. Surgery performed under magnification: _____ surgery.

5. Intentional fracturing of a bone: osteo _____ .

6. Removal of tissue for examination: bi _____ .

7. Examination of tissue using a fluoroscope: _____ scopy.

8. Suture of the loins: laparo _____ .

9. Diagnosis using x-rays: _____ diagnosis.

10. Puncture into the amniotic sac: amnio _____ .

11. Surgical alteration of the nose: rhino _____ .

12. Destruction of nerve tissue by electricity: _____ neurolysis.

13. Surgical repair of the breast: mammo _____ .

14. Motion picture of organ movement by x-ray: _____ cinematography.

15. Radiograph of a blood vessel: angio _____ .

16. Tiny suture material: _____ suture.

17. Slender knife for separating nerve fibers: neuro _____ .

18. Instrument that records uterine electrical activity: _____ hysterograph.

19. Incision into a vein: phlebo _____ .

20. Imaging of the breast by x-ray: mammo _____ .

Chapter 20 Terms in Psychiatry

The chapter on terms in psychiatry examines mental disorders in depth. The following suggestions provide specific class activities. For instructors involved in distance learning, you may want to assign some of these as self-directed student activities.

1. **Building Vocabulary**—Have each student make a flash card for each combining form and suffix on page 648 of the textbook. Each flash card should show the combining form or suffix on the front and have the definition and at least two examples on the back. See page viii of this manual for instructions.

2. **Using Resources**—Have each student or student group choose one mental disorder and discuss its symptoms and treatment. Instruct them to use the library and the Internet to list the characteristics of the disease they have chosen to discuss. Have them report to the class if possible.

3. **Creative Thinking**—Using the form below, have students make up a fictional medical chart for a person with the disease they chose to discuss in exercise 2. Have them list symptoms, potential treatments, and outlook.

Patient Name _____ Date _____

ID # _____ Date of Birth _____ Insurance carrier _____

Date	Time of Visit	Notes

4. **Practicing Pronunciation**—Have students read the Chapter Review list out loud either together or sequentially. Stop and correct any mistakes in pronunciation. (Self-study students and distance learners can refer to the audiotapes and CD-ROM and compare their pronunciations to the ones given.)

5. **Reinforcing Spelling**—With books closed, have students spell selected words that you read aloud to them from the Chapter Review list. Have any student who spells a word incorrectly write it on the blackboard or a piece of paper 10 times. (Self-study students and distance learners should use the audiotapes or the CD-ROM, by covering the screen and listening to the audio only, to test themselves. They should write down the words as they listen and check their spelling against the text.)

6. **Learning the Roots**—Read aloud psychiatric terms that are made up of word parts. Have students name the parts and define the words. (Self-study students and distance learners should use the Chapter Review lists to pick out words that can be divided into word parts. They should write the word parts and check them in the chapter itself or in a medical dictionary.)

7. **Using Medical Documents**—Choose a medical document from the section starting on page 91 of this Instructor's Manual. Ask students questions about the document to see if they comprehend the information. (Supply distance learners with a medical document and have them fill out as much as they can, providing information for a person with a psychiatric disorder.)

8. **Learning Terms**—Have students watch a medically oriented television show and listen for at least three medical terms (preferably about psychiatry). Write down the terms and their meanings.

9. **Building a Case Study**—As an end-of-chapter project, have the class build a case study. They can start with a patient with substance abuse. Have them build part of the patient's file showing doctor's notes, tests requested, results, and treatments. Each student may be assigned a role in the development of the case study. (Self-study students or distance learners can use the Internet to write a short part of a case study about a patient with a particular substance abuse problem.)

10. **Newsworthy Notes**—Have each student bring in one newspaper article (or even advertisement) or an Internet printout about substance abuse. Students should discuss the article briefly in class.

Chapter 20: Word-Building Test (20 questions—5 pts. each)

Using the following combining forms and suffixes, complete the word that best fits the definition of each word relating to terms in psychiatry listed below. Combining forms may be used more than once.

hypn(o)   -phobia
-mania   -phoria
neur(o)   psych(o)
-philia   schiz(o)

1. Destruction of neurons: _____ cytolysis.

2. Characteristic of schizophrenia: _____ oid.

3. Embryonic nerve cell: _____ blast.

4. Study of relationship of biology and psychology: _____ biology.

5. Obsessed with sexual thoughts or behavior: eroto _____ .

6. Extreme attraction for the dead: necro _____ .

7. Induction of sleep: _____ genesis.

8. Feeling of well-being: eu _____ .

9. Relationship to the mental perception of sound: _____ auditory.

10. Functional nervous condition: _____ osis.

11. General ill feeling: dys _____ .

12. Fear of bees: api _____ .

13. Fear of heights: acro _____ .

14. Treating with trancelike sleep: _____ therapy.

15. Abnormal attraction to children: pedo _____ .

16. Mild mental behavioral disorder: _____ neurosis.

17. Fear of public places: agora _____ .

18. Fear of night: nycto _____ .

19. Study of the brain and behavior: _____ psychology.

20. Using hypnosis during dental procedures: _____ odontics.

Chapter 21 Terms in Dental Practice

The chapter on terms in dental practice examines teeth and dentistry. The following suggestions provide specific class activities. For instructors involved in distance learning, you may want to assign some of these as self-directed student activities.

1. **Building Vocabulary**—Have each student make a flash card for each combining form on page 663 of the textbook. Each flash card should show the combining form on the front and have the definition and at least two examples on the back. See page viii of this manual for instructions.

2. **Using Resources**—Have each student or student group choose one tooth or gum disorder and discuss its symptoms and treatment. Instruct them to use the library and the Internet to list the characteristics of the disorder they have chosen to discuss. Have them report to the class if possible.

3. **Creative Thinking**—Using Figure 21.2 of the textbook, have students fill in notes about their own teeth—which ones have fillings, which ones have been pulled, and so on.

4. **Practicing Pronunciation**—Have students read the Chapter Review list out loud either together or sequentially. Stop and correct any mistakes in pronunciation. (Self-study students and distance learners can refer to the audiotapes and CD-ROM and compare their pronunciations to the ones given.)

5. **Reinforcing Spelling**—With books closed, have students spell selected words that you read aloud to them from the Chapter Review list. Have any student who spells a word incorrectly write it on the blackboard or a piece of paper 10 times. (Self-study students and distance learners should use the audiotapes or the CD-ROM, by covering the screen and listening to the audio only, to test themselves. They should write down the words as they listen and check their spelling against the text.)

6. **Learning the Roots**—Read aloud dental terms that are made up of word parts. Have students name the parts and define the words. (Self-study students and distance learners should use the Chapter Review lists to pick out words that can be divided into word parts. They should write the word parts and check them in the chapter itself or in a medical dictionary.)

7. **Using Medical Documents**—Choose a medical document from the section starting on page 91 of this Instructor's Manual. Ask students questions about the document to see if they comprehend the information. (Supply distance learners with a medical document and have them fill out as much as they can, providing information for a person with a dental problem.)

8. **Learning Terms**—Have students watch a medically oriented television show and listen for at least three medical terms (preferably about dentistry). Write down the terms and their meanings.

9. **Building a Case Study**—As an end-of-chapter project, have the class build a case study. They can start with a dental procedure. Have them build part of the patient's file showing dentist's notes, tests requested, results, and treatments. Each student may be assigned a role in the development of the case study. (Self-study students or distance learners can use the Internet to write a short part of a case study about a patient with a particular dental problem.)

10. **Newsworthy Notes**—Have each student bring in one newspaper article (or even advertisement) or an Internet printout about dentistry. Students should discuss the article briefly in class.

Chapter 21: Test of Dental Terms (20 questions—5 pts. each)

Complete the following sentences using a word relating to terms in dental practice.

1. The gums are also known as _____ .

2. Secondary teeth are _____ teeth.

3. The two teeth on either side of the center line of the jaw, top and bottom,
   are the _____ .

4. The white outer covering of each tooth is the _____ .

5. Specialists in the treatment of gum disease are _____ .

6. The third molar is popularly known as the _____ tooth.

7. Primary teeth are _____ teeth.

8. Cavities are usually filled with _____ .

9. Dental prostheses are _____ .

10. Dentists who specialize in treating children are _____ .

11. A missing tooth may be replaced by a bridge or a(n) _____ .

12. A toothache is called _____ .

13. Washing the mouth with a _____ solution may prevent decay.

14. The central portion of the tooth is the _____ .

15. An infection of the soft tissue of the jaw is a(n) _____ .

16. Malocclusions may be corrected with _____ .

17. The part of the tooth projecting above the jawline is the _____ .

18. TMJ dysfunction can cause _____ in the jaw.

19. A local anesthetic commonly injected prior to dental work is _____ .

20. A gas used as a dental anesthetic is _____ oxide.

Chapter 22 Terms in Pharmacology

The chapter on terms in pharmacology discusses the types, functions, and administration of pharmacological substances. The following suggestions provide specific class activities. For instructors involved in distance learning, you may want to assign some of these as self-directed student activities.

1. **Building Vocabulary**—Have each student make a flash card for each combining form on page 682 of the textbook. Each flash card should show the combining form on the front and have the definition and at least two examples on the back. See page viii of this manual for instructions.

2. **Using Resources**—Have each student or student group choose one class of drugs and discuss its purposes and some specific medications. Instruct them to use the library and the Internet to list the characteristics of the drug class they have chosen to discuss. Have them report to the class if possible.

3. **Creative Thinking**—Have students watch for television, newspaper, and magazine advertising about specific medications. Have them discuss the ethics of drug advertising and the influence that drug companies have in the prescribing of specific medications.

4. **Practicing Pronunciation**—Have students read the Chapter Review list out loud either together or sequentially. Stop and correct any mistakes in pronunciation. (Self-study students and distance learners can refer to the audiotapes and CD-ROM and compare their pronunciations to the ones given.)

5. **Reinforcing Spelling**—With books closed, have students spell selected words that you read aloud to them from the Chapter Review list. Have any student who spells a word incorrectly write it on the blackboard or a piece of paper 10 times. (Self-study students and distance learners should use the audiotapes or the CD-ROM, by covering the screen and listening to the audio only, to test themselves. They should write down the words as they listen and check their spelling against the text.)

6. **Learning the Roots**—Read aloud pharmacological terms that are made up of word parts. Have students name the parts and define the words. (Self-study students and distance learners should use the Chapter Review lists to pick out words that can be divided into word parts. They should write the word parts and check them in the chapter itself or in a medical dictionary.)

7. **Using Medical Documents**—Choose a medical document from the section starting on page 91 of this Instructor's Manual. Ask students questions about the document to see if they comprehend the information. (Supply distance learners with a medical document and have them fill out as much as they can providing information for prescriptions ordered.)

8. **Learning Terms**—Have students watch a medically oriented television show and listen for at least three medical terms (preferably about pharmacology). Write down the terms and their meanings.

9. **Building a Case Study**—As an end-of-chapter project, have the class build a case study. They can start with a patient who takes multiple medications. Have them list the patient's disorder and the prescriptions that the doctor has ordered. Each student may be assigned a role in the development of the case study. (Self-study students or distance learners can use the Internet to write a short part of a case study about a patient with a particular medical problem and a prescription that might be ordered for it.)

10. **Newsworthy Notes**—Have each student bring in one newspaper article (or even advertisement) or an Internet printout about pharmacology. Students should discuss the article briefly in class.

Name _____ Date _____

Chapter 22:   Pharmacology Test (25 questions—4 pts. each)

Give the full meaning of each abbreviation for these terms in pharmacology.

1. FDA _____

2. PDR _____

3. gr _____

4. disp. _____

5. p.o. _____

6. NPO _____

7. BID _____

8. DAW _____

9. Dx _____

10. ext. _____

11. q.d. _____

12. mg _____

13. IV _____

14. H _____

15. cap. _____

16. comp. _____

17. a.u. _____

18. aa _____

19. non. rep. _____

20. qam _____

21. p.c. _____

22. tab. _____

23. Rx _____

24. u.d. _____

25. sol. _____

Answer Key

Chapter 1: Test of Pluralizing

1. carcinomas
2. frenula
3. sera or serums
4. psychoses
5. viruses
6. septa or septums
7. femurs
8. kidneys
9. tongues
10. urethras or urethrae
11. ureters
12. malignancies
13. leukocytes
14. nuclei or nucleuses
15. reflexes
16. tremors
17. venograms
18. sutures
19. maculae or maculas
20. thrombi
21. tricuspids
22. respirations
23. antibiotics
24. fungi or funguses
25. palates

Chapter 2: Word-Building Test

1. neuralgia
2. osteoplasty
3. pathology
4. neurasthenia
5. megacephaly
6. cardiomegaly
7. litholytic
8. bacteriogenic
9. ambilateral
10. lymphocyte
11. cytocide
12. rhinoplasty
13. autophilia
14. thermogenesis
15. chromocyte
16. podalgia
17. gynopathy
18. antihemorrhagic
19. photophobia
20. rhinorrhea

Chapter 3: Word-Building Test

1. gastritis
2. lipedema
3. enterorrhaphy
4. somatalgia
5. arthropathy
6. phlebotomy
7. hidrosis
8. ophthalmoscope
9. angioplasty
10. cerebrospinal
11. osteoclasis
12. keratopathy
13. orofacial
14. pneumoresection
15. myoma
16. aortitis
17. laryngotomy
18. medullectomy
19. craniomalacia
20. enteropexy

Chapter 4: Word-Building Test

1. dermostenosis
2. mycology
3. onychomalacia
4. dermatorrhea
5. lipopenia
6. steatitis
7. xanthoderma
8. adipocyte or lipocyte
9. melanoleukoderma
10. xerosis
11. keratoplasia
12. onychophagia
13. dermabrasion
14. xerochilia
15. ichthyoid
16. xanthoma
17. trichoscopy
18. seborrhea
19. mycosis
20. ichthyosis

Chapter 5: Word-Building Test

1. myelopoiesis
2. brachiocephalic
3. ulnad
4. acetabuloplasty
5. calcipenia
6. laminitis
7. scapulopexy
8. fibrocyst

9. patellalgia
10. sternopericardial
11. dactyledema
12. lumbocostal
13. cervicobrachial
14. radiohumeral
15. kyphotone
16. pedicure
17. synovitis
18. dactylospasm
19. costosuperior
20. cervicodynia

Chapter 6: Word-Building Test

1. thrombolysis
2. pericarditis
3. cardiothrombus
4. atherogenesis
5. cardioplegia
6. arteriosclerosis
7. venosclerosis or phlebosclerosis
8. aortography
9. sphygmopalpation
10. pericardiorrhaphy
11. angiology
12. arteriopathy
13. angioid
14. cardiorrhexis
15. vasoconstrictor
16. thrombosis
17. cardiotomy
18. arteriopalmus
19. atriomegaly
20. aortostenosis

Chapter 7: Word-Building Test

1. epiglottic
2. alveoloclasia
3. lobotomy
4. phonasthenia
5. bronchitis
6. spirograph
7. pleuroclysis
8. nasosinusitis
9. thoracotomy
10. adenoidectomy
11. phrenoplegia
12. laryngotracheitis
13. oxide
14. bronchorrhea
15. capnogram
16. mediastinoscope
17. lobitis
18. bronchiostenosis
19. tracheorrhagia
20. laryngectomy

Chapter 8: Word-Building Test

1. cerebrovascular
2. glioblast
3. cranioplasty
4. encephalosclerosis
5. meningoencephalomyelitis
6. cerebellitis
7. thalamocortical
8. neuralgia
9. gangliolysis
10. encephalomyelitis
11. ventriculostomy
12. cerebrospinal
13. vagotropic
14. neuropharmacology
15. craniometer
16. vagomimetic
17. meningorrhagia
18. cerebrotomy
19. neurosurgery
20. gangliform

Chapter 9: Word-Building Test

1. glomerulopathy
2. cystitis or trigonitis
3. nephromegaly
4. cystolithotomy
5. meatoscope
6. uremia
7. calicoplasty or calioplasty
8. urethrostenosis
9. nephroma
10. cystocele or vesicocele
11. urology
12. meatoplasty
13. cystorrhaphy
14. calicotomy or caliotomy
15. renogastric
16. pyelofluoroscopy
17. cystourethritis
18. nephrosis
19. meatorrhaphy
20. glomuleronephritis

Chapter 10: Word-Building Test

1. colpopoiesis
2. menoschesis
3. mammography
4. episiostenosis
5. perineocele
6. oviform
7. salpingocyesis
8. cervicovesical
9. vaginomycosis
10. episiotomy
11. vulvitis
12. metrorrhea
13. gynecology
14. vaginodynia or colpodynia
15. oocyte
16. galactorrhea or lactorrhea
17. oophorrhagia
18. metrosalpingitis
19. menophania
20. amniocentesis

Chapter 11: Word-Building Test

1. androblastoma
2. orchiochorea
3. epididymectomy
4. balanitis
5. prostatomegaly
6. orchiopexy
7. androgyny
8. prostatocystitis
9. orchiotomy
10. prostatolith
11. epididymovasectomy
12. spermatophore
13. androgen
14. spermatolysis or spermolysis
15. orchitis or orchiditis
16. epididymotomy
17. spermatogonium
18. balanoplasty
19. spermatocide or spermicide
20. prostatorrhea

Chapter 12: Word-Building Test

1. eosinopenia
2. hemocatharsis
3. hematocystis
4. erythropoiesis
5. leukocyte
6. agglutinogenic
7. hematomyelia
8. erythropsia
9. leukapheresis
10. erythroderma
11. phagoctye
12. hemodialysis
13. erythrogenic
14. hematology
15. erythrophagia
16. thrombophlebitis
17. phagophobia
18. erythroclasis
19. thrombonecrosis
20. leukemia

Chapter 13: Word-Building Test

1. lymphocyte
2. immunosuppressant
3. lymphadenography
4. lymphuria
5. adenoma
6. splenocele
7. lymphokinesis
8. thymocyte
9. lymphadenitis
10. immunotherapy
11. thymoma
12. lymphostasis
13. toxicophobia or toxiphobia
14. adenocyte
15. toxophil
16. lymphopoiesis
17. toxiferous
18. adenomyoma
19. toxanemia
20. splenomegaly

Chapter 14: Word-Building Test

1. biligenic
2. hepatofugal
3. glucokinetic
4. enterotropic
5. cecopexy
6. labiochorea
7. cholelith
8. rectocele
9. enterostenosis
10. anoderm
11. gastrocolitis
12. stomatopathy
13. cholangioma
14. sigmoidostomy
15. appendectomy
16. hepatotoxic
17. steatorrhea
18. gastrectasis
19. colonscopy
20. stomatalgia

Chapter 15: Word-Building Test

1. glucogenesis
2. pancreatolith
3. adenectomy
4. thyrolytic
5. gonadal
6. gonadectomy
7. adrenomegaly
8. thyroiditis
9. pancreatotropic
10. thyroplasty
11. adenoma
12. adenomyoma
13. pancreatogenic
14. thyrotomy
15. adrenalitis
16. pancreatography
17. thyropathy
18. adenoblast
19. thyrotropic
20. adenolymphoma

Chapter 16: Word-Building Test

1. corectopia
2. myringotomy
3. phacocele
4. audiogenic
5. cochlear
6. nasogastric
7. dacryorrhea
8. conjunctivitis
9. retinopiesis
10. blepharedema
11. scleroplasty
12. phacomalacia
13. nasosinusitis
14. ceruminolytic
15. uveitis
16. iritis
17. ophthalmomycosis
18. dacryostenosis
19. scotopic
20. ossiculectomy

Chapter 17: Test of the Stages of Human Development

1. toddler
2. fertilization
3. middle
4. embryo
5. puberty
6. gerontology
7. 90
8. fetus
9. cephalic
10. breech
11. old age
12. obstetricians
13. secondary
14. neonate
15. labor
16. vaginal
17. adolescence
18. cesarean section
19. gestation
20. neonatologists

Chapter 18: Word-Building Test

1. oncogenic
2. mutagen
3. blastoma
4. dysplasia
5. radiology
6. carcinostatic
7. carcinolytic
8. radiotoxemia
9. neuroblastoma
10. oncocyte
11. radiotherapy
12. cytoplasm
13. neoplasm
14. blastocyte
15. radiometer
16. oncolytic
17. dysplasia
18. blastogenesis
19. radiodiagnosis
20. oncotherapy

Chapter 19: Word-Building Test

1. myectomy
2. colostomy
3. cardiogram
4. microsurgery
5. osteoclasis
6. biopsy
7. fluoroscopy
8. laparorrhaphy
9. radiodiagnosis
10. amniocentesis
11. rhinoplasty
12. electroneurolysis
13. mammoplasty
14. radiocinematography
15. angiogram
16. microsuture
17. neurotome
18. electrohysterograph
19. phlebotomy
20. mammography

Chapter 20: Word-Building Test

1. neurocytolysis
2. schizoid
3. neuroblast
4. psychobiology
5. erotomania
6. necrophilia
7. hypnogenesis
8. euphoria
9. psychoauditory
10. neurosis
11. dysphoria
12. apiphobia
13. acrophobia
14. hypnotherapy
15. pedophilia
16. psychoneurosis
17. agoraphobia
18. nyctophobia
19. neuropsychology
20. hypnodontics

Chapter 21: Test of Dental Terms

1. gingivae
2. permanent
3. central incisors
4. enamel
5. periodontists
6. wisdom
7. deciduous
8. amalgam
9. dentures
10. pedodontists
11. implant
12. odontalgia
13. fluoride
14. pulp cavity
15. abscess
16. braces
17. crown
18. pain
19. Novacaine
20. nitrous

Chapter 22: Pharmacology Test

1. Food and Drug Administration
2. Physician's Desk Reference
3. gram
4. dispense
5. by mouth
6. nothing by mouth
7. twice a day
8. dispense as written
9. diagnosis
10. extract
11. every day
12. milligram
13. intravenous
14. hypodermic
15. capsule
16. compound
17. each ear
18. of each
19. do not repeat
20. every morning
21. after meals
22. tablet
23. prescription
24. as directed
25. solution

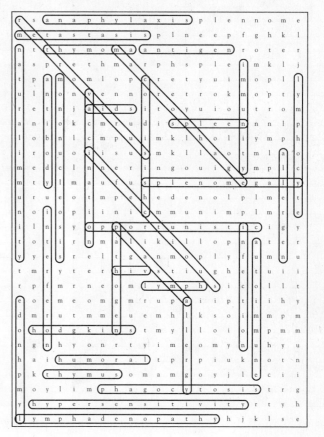

Answers to Figure 13.1

Answers to Figure 5.1

Answers to Figure 6.1

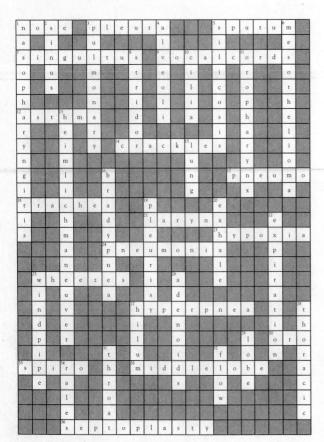

Answers to Figure 7.1

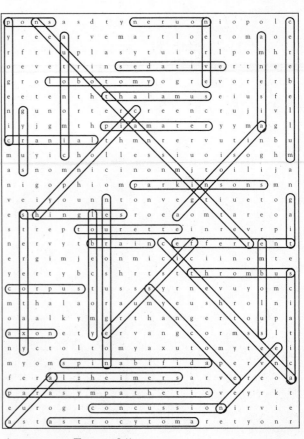

Answers to Figure 8.1

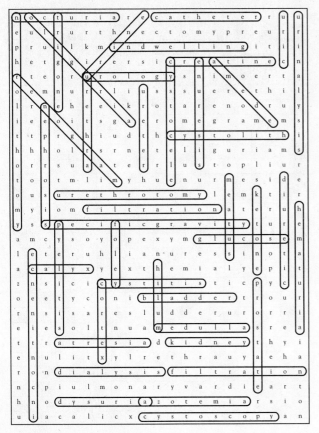

Answers to Figure 9.1

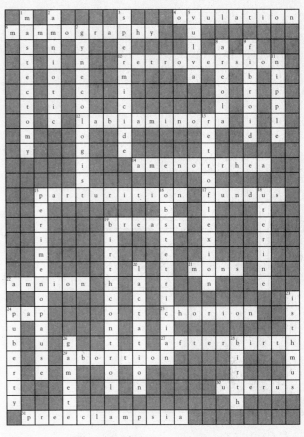

Answers to Figure 10.1

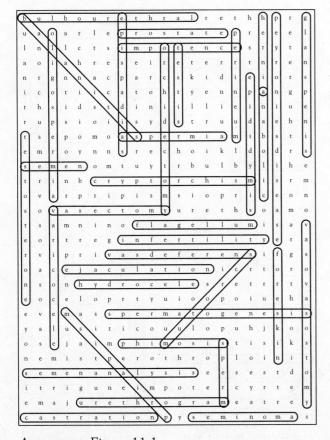

Answers to Figure 11.1

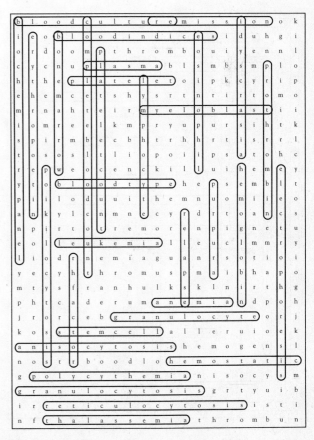

Answers to Figure 12.1

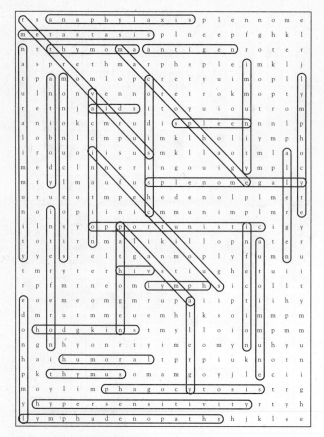

Answers to Figure 13.1

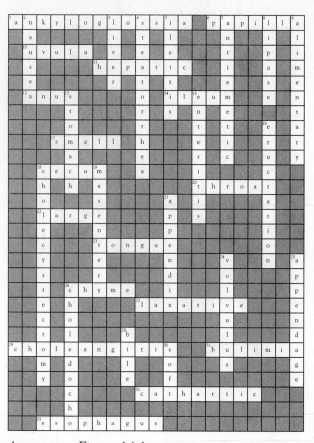

Answers to Figure 14.1

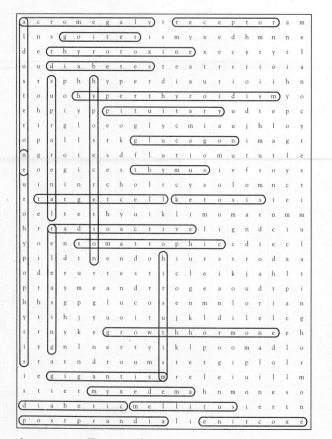

Answers to Figure 15.1

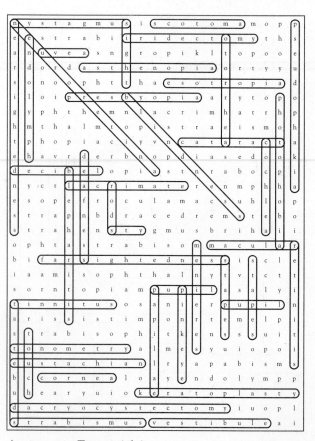

Answers to Figure 16.1

Medical Documents

PLEASE
DO NOT
STAPLE
IN THIS
AREA

CARRIER

| | | PICA | | | | **HEALTH INSURANCE CLAIM FORM** | PICA | | |

1. MEDICARE MEDICAID CHAMPUS CHAMPVA GROUP HEALTH PLAN FECA BLK LUNG OTHER
(Medicare #) (Medicaid #) (Sponsor's SSN) (VA File #) (SSN or ID) (SSN) (ID)

1a. INSURED'S I.D. NUMBER (FOR PROGRAM IN ITEM 1)

2. PATIENT'S NAME (Last Name, First Name, Middle Initial)

3. PATIENT'S BIRTH DATE MM DD YY SEX M F

4. INSURED'S NAME (Last Name, First Name, Middle Initial)

5. PATIENT'S ADDRESS (No., Street)

6. PATIENT RELATIONSHIP TO INSURED Self Spouse Child Other

7. INSURED'S ADDRESS (No., Street)

CITY STATE

8. PATIENT STATUS Single Married Other
Employed Full-Time Student Part-Time Student

CITY STATE

ZIP CODE TELEPHONE (Include Area Code) (   )

ZIP CODE TELEPHONE (INCLUDE AREA CODE) (   )

9. OTHER INSURED'S NAME (Last Name, First Name, Middle Initial)

10. IS PATIENT'S CONDITION RELATED TO:

11. INSURED'S POLICY GROUP OR FECA NUMBER

a. OTHER INSURED'S POLICY OR GROUP NUMBER

a. EMPLOYMENT? (CURRENT OR PREVIOUS) YES NO

a. INSURED'S DATE OF BIRTH MM DD YY SEX M F

b. OTHER INSURED'S DATE OF BIRTH MM DD YY SEX M F

b. AUTO ACCIDENT? PLACE (State) YES NO

b. EMPLOYER'S NAME OR SCHOOL NAME

c. EMPLOYER'S NAME OR SCHOOL NAME

c. OTHER ACCIDENT? YES NO

c. INSURANCE PLAN NAME OR PROGRAM NAME

d. INSURANCE PLAN NAME OR PROGRAM NAME

10d. RESERVED FOR LOCAL USE

d. IS THERE ANOTHER HEALTH BENEFIT PLAN? YES NO If yes, return to and complete item 9 a-d.

READ BACK OF FORM BEFORE COMPLETING & SIGNING THIS FORM.

12. PATIENT'S OR AUTHORIZED PERSON'S SIGNATURE I authorize the release of any medical or other information necessary to process this claim. I also request payment of government benefits either to myself or to the party who accepts assignment below.

SIGNED _____ DATE _____

13. INSURED'S OR AUTHORIZED PERSON'S SIGNATURE I authorize payment of medical benefits to the undersigned physician or supplier for services described below.

SIGNED _____

PATIENT AND INSURED INFORMATION

14. DATE OF CURRENT: ILLNESS (First symptom) OR INJURY (Accident) OR PREGNANCY (LMP) MM DD YY

15. IF PATIENT HAS HAD SAME OR SIMILAR ILLNESS, GIVE FIRST DATE MM DD YY

16. DATES PATIENT UNABLE TO WORK IN CURRENT OCCUPATION FROM MM DD YY TO MM DD YY

17. NAME OF REFERRING PHYSICIAN OR OTHER SOURCE

17a. I.D. NUMBER OF REFERRING PHYSICIAN

18. HOSPITALIZATION DATES RELATED TO CURRENT SERVICES FROM MM DD YY TO MM DD YY

19. RESERVED FOR LOCAL USE

20. OUTSIDE LAB? YES NO $ CHARGES

21. DIAGNOSIS OR NATURE OF ILLNESS OR INJURY. (RELATE ITEMS 1,2,3, OR 4 TO ITEM 24E BY LINE)

1. _____ 3. _____

2. _____ 4. _____

22. MEDICAID RESUBMISSION CODE ORIGINAL REF. NO.

23. PRIOR AUTHORIZATION NUMBER

24. A						B	C	D			E	F	G	H	I	J	K
From DATE(S) OF SERVICE To						Place of Service	Type of Service	PROCEDURES, SERVICES, OR SUPPLIES (Explain Unusual Circumstances)			DIAGNOSIS CODE	$ CHARGES	DAYS OR UNITS	EPSDT Family Plan	EMG	COB	RESERVED FOR LOCAL USE
MM	DD	YY	MM	DD	YY			CPT/HCPCS	MODIFIER								
1																	
2																	
3																	
4																	
5																	
6																	

25. FEDERAL TAX I.D. NUMBER SSN EIN

26. PATIENT'S ACCOUNT NO.

27. ACCEPT ASSIGNMENT? (For govt. claims, see back) YES NO

28. TOTAL CHARGE $

29. AMOUNT PAID $

30. BALANCE DUE $

31. SIGNATURE OF PHYSICIAN OR SUPPLIER INCLUDING DEGREES OR CREDENTIALS (I certify that the statements on the reverse apply to this bill and are made a part thereof.)

SIGNED _____ DATE _____

32. NAME AND ADDRESS OF FACILITY WHERE SERVICES WERE RENDERED (if other than home or office)

33. PHYSICIAN'S OR SUPPLIER'S NAME, ADDRESS, ZIP CODE & TELEPHONE NO.

PIN# GRP#

PHYSICIAN OR SUPPLIER INFORMATION

(APPROVED BY AMA COUNCIL ON MEDICAL SERVICE 8/88) *PLEASE PRINT OR TYPE*

FORM HCFA-1500 (12-90)
FORM OWCP-1500 FORM RRB-1500

HCFA Form.

AUTHORIZATION TO RELEASE MEDICAL INFORMATION

Original Authorization MUST be attached to the patient's permanent medical record. A copy of this Authorization should be attached to forwarded medical record.

DATE: _____

TO: Family Medical Group
2100 Grace Avenue
Columbus, OH 43080
999-555-9800, 999-555-9801 fax

RE: _____
Patient name

_____
Patient street address

_____
Patient city, state, ZIP

_____
Patient telephone

_____
Patient date of birth

The undersigned hereby requests and authorizes Family Medical Group to release to (INSERT NAME OF RECIPIENT OF PATIENT RECORDS) or any of his/her/their assigned representatives, copies of any and all records and documents regarding the undersigned's past and current medical treatment, medical condition(s) and medical expenses. The information to be released includes any and all medical and hospital records currently within your possession, including those records which have been furnished to Family Medical Group by other physicians and medical providers, and including, but not limited to, any and all X-ray films, pathology slides, laboratory reports, medical histories, consultation reports, prescriptions, medical correspondence, consent forms, employment information, and billing information.

In addition to authorizing the release of the above stated medical records and documents, the undersigned expressly authorizes Family Medical Group to release the following information to the designated individual or entity: (Please initial the items below for release, if appropriate)

_____ Psychiatric information   _____ Drug/Alcohol information   _____ HIV-related information

Family Medical Group is instructed to comply with this request by providing *copies* of my records only, with the understanding that my original medical record will be maintained within the possession of Family Medical Group.

A copy of this authorization **shall not** be used in lieu of an originally signed authorization.

This authorization may be revoked by the undersigned at any time by a written notice to Family Medical Group except to the extent that action has already been taken.

This authorization will expire sixty (60) days from the date of this request OR _____ (specify other date) and will be null and void thereafter.

_____   _____
Signature of patient   Date

Patient is a minor, or patient is legally unable to sign because   _____

_____   _____
Signature of authorized person   Date

_____   _____
Print name of authorized person   Relationship to patient

Disclosure statement: This information is being disclosed to you from records whose confidentiality is protected by Federal and State Law. Federal and State Law prohibit you from making any further disclosure of this information without the specific written authorization of the person to whom it pertains, or as otherwise permitted by Law.

Release of information form.

PATIENT INFORMATION FORM

THIS SECTION REFERS TO PATIENT ONLY

Name:	Sex:	Marital status: □ S □ M □ D □ W	Birth date:

Address: | SS#:

City: State: Zip: | Employer:

Home phone: | Employer's address:

Work phone: | City: State: Zip:

Spouse's name: | Spouse's employer:

Emergency contact: | Relationship: Phone #:

FILL IN IF PATIENT IS A MINOR

Parent/Guardian's name:	Sex:	Marital status: □ S □ M □ D □ W	Birth date:

Phone: | SS#:

Address: | Employer:

City: State: Zip: | Employer's address:

Student status: | City: State: Zip:

INSURANCE INFORMATION

Primary insurance company: | Secondary insurance company:

Policyholder's name: Birth date: | Policyholder's name: Birth date:

Plan: SS#: | Plan:

Policy #:   Group #: | Policy #:   Group #:

OTHER INFORMATION

Reason for visit: | Allergy to medication (list):

Name of referring physician: | If auto accident, list date and state in which it occurred:

_____   _____

(Patient's signature/Parent or guardian's signature)   (Date)

Patient information form.

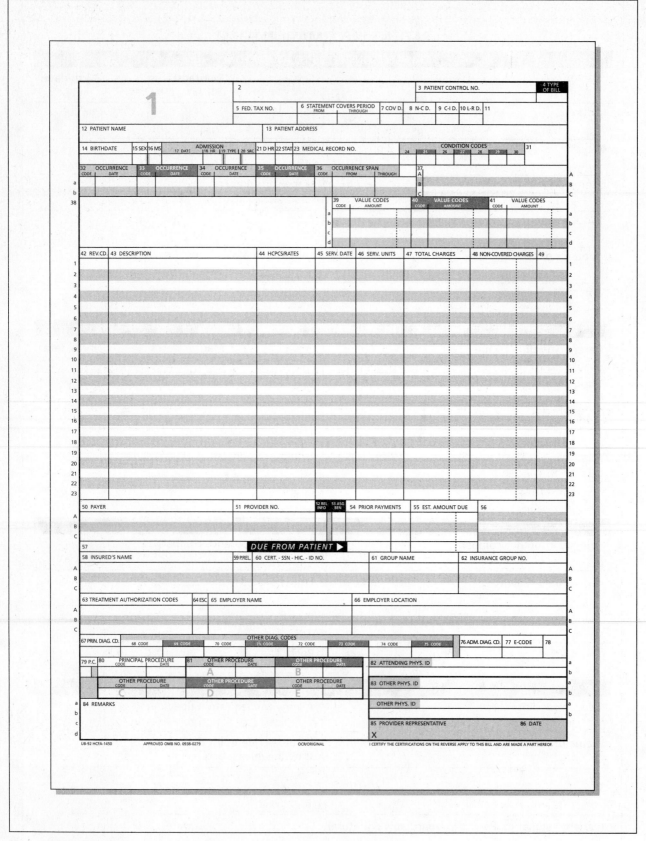

Hospital billing claim form.

VALLEY ASSOCIATES, P.C.
Christopher M. Connolly, M.D. - Internal Medicine
555-967-0303
FED I.D. #16-1234567

PATIENT NAME	APPT. DATE/TIME
Deysenrothe, Mae J.	10/06/2003 9:30am

PATIENT NO.	DX
DEYSEMA0	**1.** V70.0 Exam, Adult **2.** **3.** **4.**

DESCRIPTION	✓	CPT	FEE	DESCRIPTION	✓	CPT	FEE
EXAMINATION				**PROCEDURES**			
New Patient				Anoscopy; diagnostic		46600	
Problem Focused		99201		ECG w/Interpretation		93000	
Expanded Problem Focused		99202		ECG, Rhythm, w/Interp.		93040	
Detailed		99203		I&D, Abscess		10060	
Comprehensive		99204		Pap Smear		88150	
Comprehensive/Complex		99205		Pap Smear, Screening, MC		Q0091	
Established Patient				Removal of Cerumen		69210	
Minimum		99211		Removal 1 Lesion		17000*	
Problem Focused		99212		Removal 2-14 Lesions		+17003	
Expanded Problem Focused		99213		Removal 15+ Lesions		17004	
Detailed		99214		Sigmoidoscopy, Flex.		45330	
Comprehensive/Complex		99215					
				LABORATORY			
PREVENTIVE VISIT				Glucose Finger Stick		82948	
New Patient				Specimen Handling		99000	
Age 12-17		99384		Stool/Occult Blood		82270	
Age 18-39		99385		Tine Test		85585	
Age 40-64		99386		Tuberculin PPD		85580	
Age 65+		99387		Urinalysis		81000	
Established Patient				Venipuncture		36415	
Age 12-17		99394		Venipuncture MC		G0001	
Age 18-39		99395					
Age 40-64		99396		**INJECTION/IMMUN.**			
Age 65+		99397		B12 Injection (J3420)		90752	
				DT		90702	
CONSULTATION: OFFICE/ER				Hepatitis A		90730	
Requested By:				Hepatitis B		90746	
Problem Focused		99241		Influenza		90724	
Expanded Problem Focused		99242		Influenza MC		G0008	
Detailed		99243		Pneumovax		90732	
Comprehensive		99244		Pneumovax MC		G0009	
Comprehensive/Complex		99245					
				TOTAL FEES			

Encounter form.

DATE/TIME	

Patient name _____ Age _____ Current Diagnosis _____

Patient record form.